At My Grandmother's Table

Heartwarming Stories & Cherished Recipes from the South

Faye Porter

THOMAS NELSON
Since 1798

NASHVILLE   DALLAS   MEXICO CITY   RIO DE JANEIRO

Published in Nashville, Tennessee, by Thomas Nelson. Thomas Nelson is a trademark of Thomas Nelson, Inc.

Photography by Stephanie Mullins

Food Styling by Teresa Blackburn

Dishes used on pages 28, 79, 146, 172, and 219 courtesy of the Mosley family, in loving memory of Margaret Mosley.

Bean pot used on page 100 courtesy of Lea Mosley.

Thomas Nelson, Inc., titles may be purchased in bulk for educational, business, fund-raising, or sales promotional use. For information, please e-mail SpecialMarkets@ThomasNelson.com.

The Library of Congress Cataloging-in-Publication Data

Porter, Faye, 1966-
  At my grandmother's table : heartwarming stories and cherished recipes from the South / Faye Porter.
    pages cm
  Includes index.
  ISBN 978-1-4016-0488-2
  1. Cooking, American--Southern style. I. Title.
  TX715.2.S68P675 2013
  641.5975--dc23

2012042581

Printed in the United States of America

13 14 15 16 17 QG 6 5 4 3 2 1

To my niece and godchild, Lillian Porter, and her sweet
reminder that every day is a great day to be alive . . .

Contents

Introduction

Oftentimes we like what we like because it's what we know. And what we know is based on the experiences and traditions we learned growing up. So many of our best memories and time-honored traditions are wrapped up in food and time spent with loved ones around the table. While table time these days does not occur often for many on-the-go families, one thing is certain—you can always count on having a place set for you at the table of a Southern grandmother. It's these quintessential ladies who continue to make sure that the art of entertaining stays alive and well in homes throughout the South.

When *At My Grandmother's Knee* was published in 2011, a number of readers shared that they sat down with their copy, intending to look for a recipe, but instead ended up reading it from cover to cover because they loved the stories. And as we found out in interviewing ladies for that book, there were just as many Southern men who, on the spot, could recall their memories of Grandma and the much-loved food she made, and wished they could participate. So *At My Grandmother's Table* was born—this edition based on the same theme, but featuring both Southern grandsons and granddaughters reminiscing about their beloved family matriarchs, whether known best to them as Nana, Grana, Memaw, or just simply Grandma.

Ideally, the love of a grandmother is pure and unconditional, spoken uniquely throughout her life with countless gestures—often by what she creates with her hands and heart. Some of us have tangible keepsakes handmade by our grandmothers—quilts, blankets, doll clothes, etc.—yet for most of us the keepsakes are intangible, built on years of rich memories made at the table with loved ones around it. There will always be certain foods, scents, sights, and sounds that can transport us right back to our places at our grandmas' tables or helping in their kitchens. Our senses can evoke such sweet thoughts of those incredible Southern dishes that have become our favorites—it's no wonder then that this cuisine is best described as comfort food! Most Southern grandmas will agree—there is no greater way to show their love for family and friends than with their special gift of hosting a meal or gathering, complete with all the homemade fixins.

What comes to mind when you think of your grandmother's table? Who is sitting around it? What's on it? . . . For me, the smell of a long-baked ham or a beef roast with carrots and potatoes reminds me of a Sunday afternoon at my Grandma Porter's house. Also on the table would be high-rise homemade dinner rolls, a crystal dish with dark green lime pickles, homemade noodles, and a mile-high angel food cake with maple icing for dessert. At Grandma Ferkan's, it would be her giant sugar cookies inside the big apple cookie jar, homemade haluski with cheese dumplings in the tan and brown–speckled bowl, and mint ginger ale served over ice in white and color–striped glasses—all prepared with my Aunt Emma in the kitchen.

I lost my last grandparent at the age of ten. How I've longed for more time with any of them. While certainly not a replacement, I fortunately had my parents, brothers, many aunts and uncles, and older cousins who could help fill in some of the missing details. It's through old pictures, letters, recipes, and stories passed down that we can carry on the traditions of our loved ones and introduce those traditions to new generations.

I'm grateful for maternal cousins Debbie, Carol, and Larry, who have been assembling recipes to archive our family favorites. And for those of us becoming the new older genera-tion in our families, may we always value the importance of a legacy and carrying on the traditions of those who came before us by celebrating life events, honoring a life passed, or getting together "just because." I don't know about your gatherings, but for us, regardless of the occasion, it becomes story time—keeping the past alive by sharing old ones and creating new memories that just might become tomorrow's retold gems.

Whether you're lucky enough to still be invited by your grandma or if you're now part of the next generation doing the inviting, it's important that we continue to come together and celebrate when we can—both to showcase our time-honored rituals and traditions for younger generations and to create new experiences for stories yet untold.

And, by all means, share your recipes—based on the pleasant memories that food evokes, you can honor a special someone every time you re-create her famous dish.

So grab your iced tea, sit back, and join me—page by page—at the tables of these treasured Southern grandmothers. Enjoy!

FAYE PORTER

Kentucky-Style Southern Sweet Tea

Mimi's Hot Tea

Lemonade-Strawberry Punch

Mamo May's 1920s-Style Christmas Float

B. G.'s Lemon Tea Fizz

Great K. K.'s Strawberry Lemonade

Beverages

KENTUCKY-STYLE SOUTHERN SWEET TEA

KRISTIN CEDERLIND currently lives in Las Vegas, Nevada, but she comes from a long line of Southerners, including her parents and grandparents. Kristin visits the South often and shares that her grandmother, **DOROTHY HURST** (Ashland, Kentucky), used to always make her Southern-style sweet tea for the family when they would visit and sit on the porch. Grandma served this tea in her beautiful Pilgrim Glass glasses and would always say, "Be very careful, honey—don't break Grandma's special iced tea glass; hold it with both hands." Kristin says that her grandma's tea was always made with love, and she still uses her grandmother's recipe to this day.

6 to 8 tea bags	1 cup sugar	Sprigs of mint
6 cups water	2 to 3 oranges, sliced	

1 In a large pot, add the tea bags and water. Bring to a rolling boil, remove from the heat, and let steep 5 minutes. Remove the tea bags.
2 Pour the liquid into a gallon jug and add cold water to fill. Add the sugar (you can add more if you want sweeter tea). Add the oranges and mint and stir. Pour over ice and enjoy.

MAKES 1 GALLON.

⟨✕✕✕ MIMI'S HOT TEA

LAUREL STANDIFER (Franklin, Tennessee) was born in Dothan, Alabama. Her grand-mother was affectionately known as Mimi. Mimi was HELON BARRON STANDIFER (Dothan, Alabama), who was born in Panama City, Florida. Growing up, Mimi was very poor, one of six children. Laurel shares that "Mimi told us how she would hide in the bathroom sometimes during school lunch because she didn't have food to eat. I think this may have helped to develop her love for cooking as she grew up. Out of all her siblings, Mimi was known as the cook of her family. She was so loving and generous, always helping and lovingly caring for our family." Sadly, she passed away in 2000.

4 medium oranges

3 lemons

2 cups sugar

I gallon water

I tablespoon black tea

I teaspoon cloves

I cinnamon stick

1 Slice the oranges and lemons thin. Place them in a large pot. Cover with the sugar and let stand I hour.

2 Bring I gallon of water to a boil over high heat. Add the tea and allow to steep for 4 to 5 minutes. Strain the tea over the fruit.

3 Add the cloves and cinnamon and bring to a simmer over medium-low heat. Allow to simmer 2 hours. Serve hot. You may add 4 tablespoons of rum, if desired, per serving.

MAKES 16 (8 OUNCE) SERVINGS.

LEMONADE-STRAWBERRY PUNCH ✕ ✕

Grandma Mac told ELIZABETH "LIB" BOWMAN HAUSER (Liberty, North Carolina) that Lib needed to learn how to make biscuits from scratch, as it was a good way to "catch a husband." Grandma Mac, ALIVIE ELIZABETH BRYAN McPHERSON, was born and raised on a dairy farm in Burlington, North Carolina. Lib has fond memories of her grandma fixing fried chicken for Sunday lunches and of her tradition of putting a pitcher of cold milk on the table when serving her homemade cookies. Grandma Mac would say, "You need a glass of milk for cookie dunkin'." Lib shares, "This punch was served at my wedding reception more than fifty years ago—and, of course at that time, wedding receptions were held in the church. To serve seventy-five people it took someone constantly mixing the punch! It was always served in a large crystal punch bowl in crystal punch cups along with cake, mints, and cake squares rounding out the menu."

1 1/2 cups fresh strawberries, hulled and sliced, divided

3 (6 ounce) cans frozen lemonade concentrate

1/2 cup sugar

2 quarts ice water

1 quart ginger ale, chilled

3 (6 ounce) cans frozen orange juice concentrate, thawed

Frozen ring of ice

1 Place half of the strawberries in a blender. Add the lemonade concentrate and the sugar and blend on low speed until mixed well, approximately 90 seconds. Let stand for 30 minutes.

2 When ready to serve, pour the ice water and ginger ale in a large punch bowl. Stir in the blended strawberry mixture and the thawed orange juice concentrate. Add the frozen ring of ice.

3 Cut the other half of the strawberries into quarters and add as garnish in the punch. Mix and enjoy. Serve cold in 4-ounce crystal punch cups.

MAKES 32 (4 OUNCE) SERVINGS.

MAMO MAY'S 1920s-STYLE CHRISTMAS FLOAT ✕ ✕

BETTY RICH NORMANT (Henderson, Kentucky) shares that her grandmother, MAGGIE MAY (Salyersville, Kentucky), was known as Mamo May. A homemaker, Mamo May and her husband, Eli, raised two daughters—Lucille and Nancy. Betty's mother was Lucille, who married Walter Rich of Lancaster, Kentucky. Following World War II, they moved from Salyersville to Union County on the opposite end of the state, where Eli began farming. While she never lived in Salyersville again, Lucille taught her daughters, Sara and Betty, to love the mountains of Kentucky. They frequently visited their grandparents and enjoyed the incredible meals that Mamo May prepared. It has been said that proposals of marriage have been made over a cup of this delicious float. Regardless, it is a favorite of all ages and evokes warm memories of the loved one who made it for you.

1 quart whole milk	Pinch of salt	Whipped cream
4 large eggs	2 teaspoons vanilla extract	Cherries (optional)
1 cup sugar		

1 Heat the milk over medium heat in a double boiler to avoid scorching. Heat but don't boil the milk.

2 Meanwhile, beat the eggs, sugar, and salt together. When the milk is hot, beat a few tablespoons of the hot milk into the egg mixture. Then add the egg mixture slowly back into the rest of the hot milk.

3 Stir continuously and cook until the mixture coats the spoon. Remove from the heat and set the pan in a larger pan of cold water and continue stirring. Add the vanilla.

4 Continue stirring to cool the mixture and smooth the texture. When cool, store in an airtight jar in the refrigerator. Serve in crystal punch cups with a dollop of whipped cream and a cherry on top.

MAKES 16 (½ CUP) SERVINGS.

NOTE: *Recipe can be doubled or tripled.*

B. G.'S LEMON TEA FIZZ

BETTY KEELING GREEN WOOTEN (Nashville, Tennessee) is known as B. G. to her six grandchildren, and to the rest of Davidson County as Judge Green. She has served as a Davidson County Juvenile Court judge for fourteen years beforing retiring in 2012. When grandson MACLAINE BUTTERS (Brentwood, Tennessee) was little, he loved to visit her at the court, which was right beside the Tennessee Titans stadium. There was always a candy dish to raid or a treat to be had. Every now and then, she would let him sit "on the bench" and bang the gavel—a dream for any kid who loves to make noise. MacLaine loves this recipe because it has two of his favorite things to drink—lemonade and Sprite!

I ½ quarts water

9 tea bags (or 3 family-size bags)

½ cup sugar

I (12 ounce) can frozen lemonade concentrate

I (12 ounce) can Sprite or other lemon-lime soda

Ice

---

1 Bring the water to a boil over high heat. Remove from the heat, add the tea bags, and brew 6 to 10 minutes. Let cool slightly and mix in the sugar until dissolved.

2 Stir in the can of frozen lemonade concentrate. Refrigerate until ready to serve. Just before serving, add the soda and mix well. Serve over ice.

MAKES 6 (8 OUNCE) SERVINGS.

GREAT K. K.'S STRAWBERRY LEMONADE ✕ ✕ ›

Growing up, siblings **ALLYSON ADAMS JOHNSON** (Hendersonville, Tennessee), **MANDY BUTTERS** (Brentwood, Tennessee), and **ANDREW HELTSLEY** (Nashville, Tennessee) would visit their grandmother, K. K.—**KATHERINE CORTNER KEELING** (Nashville, Tennessee)—in Tullahoma, Tennessee, on the weekends. They would typically find K. K. and her husband, Jackson, sitting on their front porch on East Lincoln Street, rain or shine, watching the world go by. They share that K. K. cooked huge family meals served on HUGE plates. And she kept adding to her collection. It became a joke in the family to see how much bigger in diameter the plates could even get (to hold more food)! They also used to take family trips to Florida, where the "make-your-own-fun" included theme parties (such as a toga or tacky theme) hosted by K. K. for the family in her hotel room. K. K. kept the tradition alive by taking Allyson, Mandy, and Andrew on short weekend excursions from time to time to Tennessee locations that included Henry Horton State Park or the Smokehouse in Monteagle—nothing fancy, just something to make them feel special. Now grown and married, Allyson, Mandy, and Andrew each have two children. They are so grateful their children have gotten the chance to know their beloved K. K. (The six great-grandchildren call her Great K. K.)

1 ½ cups strawberries, stems removed	1 ½ cups fresh lemon juice (5 to 6 lemons), divided	1 cup sugar
		4 cups water
		Ice

1 Puree the strawberries and 3 tablespoons of the lemon juice in a blender or food processor until smooth. Pour the puree through a sieve into a bowl to remove the seeds.

2 In a 2-quart pitcher, stir the strained puree, the remaining lemon juice, sugar, and water. Taste and add more water if desired. Serve immediately over lots of ice.

MAKES 8 (8 OUNCE) SERVINGS.

Grammy's Bacon Crescents

Selena's Favorite Jelly

Breakfast Pizza

Babe's Sunday Morning Flapjacks

Yesterday's Grits for Breakfast

Big Mama's Brunch Casserole

Tomato Breakfast Gravy

Special-Occasion French Toast

Nineteenth-Century Spice Muffins

Jules's Blueberry Sausage Casserole

Breakfast Cheese Bread

Nana's Sausage Cheese Bites

Tori's Quiche

Julesy's "Bloob-Berry" Breakfast Muffins

Granny's Fruit Compote

"Sweet as Can Be" Caramel Pecan Rolls

Grandma's Buttermilk Waffles

Old-Fashioned Doughnuts

Grandmother Caldwell's Petite Coffee Cakes

Breakfast

GRAMMY'S BACON CRESCENTS

DILLON YOUNG (Nashville, Tennessee) was born in West Palm Beach, Florida. Dillon is the first grandchild of four for his Grammy, ERNIE YOUNG. Ernie was born in Richmond, Virginia, but she now lives in Franklin, Tennessee. Ernie loves to cook and bake, and Dillon's favorite things she makes are her biscuits and her roast beef with carrots and potatoes. Ernie is also known for crocheting blankets, and Dillon, of course, has been the recipient of a couple. In 2012, as a freshman at Vanderbilt University, he received a new blanket in the Commodores' colors. Ernie says these crescents are great as an appetizer or as a breakfast treat.

1 (8 ounce) package cream cheese, softened

⅓ cup grated Parmesan cheese

¼ cup finely chopped onion

2 tablespoons chopped parsley

1 teaspoon milk (whole or 2 percent)

2 (8 ounce) cans crescent rolls

8 slices bacon, cooked and crumbled

1 Preheat the oven to 375 degrees.
2 In a medium bowl mix the cream cheese, Parmesan cheese, onion, parsley, and milk. Blend well.
3 Separate the dough into triangles. Cut each triangle in half lengthwise and spread each with the cream cheese mixture. Sprinkle with bacon and roll up. Place seam side down on a greased cookie sheet. Bake for 12 to 15 minutes or until golden brown.

MAKES 16 ROLLS.

SELENA'S FAVORITE JELLY ✕ ✕ ✕

Granddaughter **Selena Jade Seate** doesn't open her homemade biscuits, shares **Carol Ann Rupp Crawley** (Alton, Virginia); she just spreads the jelly all over the top of a whole warm one! Selena's most favorite food is homemade biscuits with freezer strawberry jelly, so this favorite is now known as "Selena Jelly" to this family. Selena and her younger sister, Brett, spent the summer of 2012 in Alton, Virginia, living with their grandparents, whom they affectionately refer to as Old Mommie and Ampy. Selena is the oldest grandchild, and she lived with her grandparents most of her first year of life, as her daddy was in the Marines, serving in Cuba. Old Mommie kept her a great deal while her mama worked evenings and weekends, so Selena started calling her Mama. No matter what other usual grandmother name they tried, Selena could not pronounce the "grrrr" sound. They explained to her that she only had one official "mommy"—so they finally decided grandma would be her "Old Mommie." And that is what Carol has been to Selena and the other eight grandkids ever since.

2 pints strawberries, cleaned, capped, and mashed (about	2 cups crushed berries)*	1 (1.75 ounce) box fruit pectin
	4 cups sugar	3/4 cup water

1 Place the strawberries in a large bowl. Add the sugar to the crushed berries and allow to sit for 10 minutes, stirring every few minutes to dissolve the sugar.

2 In a small saucepan bring the fruit pectin and water to a boil and gradually add to the berry mixture. Stir until the mixture is no longer grainy, about 3 minutes.

3 Pour the jelly into freezer-safe glass jars with tight-fitting metal lids or rigid plastic containers with tight-fitting lids, leaving 1/2-inch space at the top for expansion when frozen. Screw the lids on and let stand at room temperature for 24 hours until set. Refrigerate up to 3 weeks or freeze up to a year.

FILLS 8 (1/2 CUP) OR 4 (1 CUP) CONTAINERS.

* It's best to use the strawberries at room temperature. When preparing the berries, mash and crush with a fork or potato masher instead of a food processor, as it will puree the fruit too much. Use only the amount of fruit called for in this recipe. Using more than two cups can affect how the jelly will set.

BREAKFAST PIZZA ⊠ ⊠ ⊠

In addition to putting God and family first in her life, Grandma JOSAPHINE CATIGNANI (Nashville, Tennessee) also taught her granddaughter, SHERRIE CUNNINGHAM (Old Hickory, Tennessee), how to cook some traditional Southern and Italian favorites. While Josaphine was born and raised in the South, it was important to her to learn some of the dishes of her ancestors. She had a love of Italian spices and cooking traditional favorites too. Sherrie shares that Grandma Josaphine used to say, "When the children are little, they step on your feet, and when they are grown, they step on your heart." Sherrie indicates this pizza is a big hit with family and friends!

Vegetable shortening to prepare pan

1 (8 ounce) can crescent rolls

6 large eggs

1/2 pound sausage, browned and drained (or bacon or ham)

1/2 cup each chopped onion,

mushrooms, peppers (optional)

1 cup shredded Cheddar cheese

1 Preheat the oven to 375 degrees. Lightly grease a cookie sheet or 9 x 13-inch baking pan.
2 Place the crescent rolls on the prepared pan to form the crust, pressing the seams together and the sides up slightly.
3 Beat the eggs and pour over the crescent rolls. Add the meat and optional vegetables. Sprinkle cheese over the top.
4 Bake 25 to 30 minutes, or until the egg mixture is set. Slice with a pizza cutter and serve warm.

MAKES 8 SERVINGS.

✕✕✕ BABE'S SUNDAY MORNING FLAPJACKS

FRANCES ST. JOHN NIX LAVEY'S (Nashville, Tennessee) grandmother, MARTHA HIGHTOWER TURNER (Demopolis, Alabama), is affectionately known as Babe to her six grandchildren. Babe lives in an antebellum home in Demopolis on the high bluffs of the Tombigbee River. Frances shares, "When I visit, the smell of hot flapjacks wakes me up on Sunday mornings. My feet hit the cold wooden floorboards as I tiptoe into the warm, bright kitchen. I hear Babe humming quietly to herself as I walk up to the high linoleum counter. 'Good morning, darling,' she says in her deep Southern accent. 'Morning, Babe' is all I can manage to say because I'm half-asleep. I start mixing the ingredients for the next batch because I know once everyone else wakes up, these pancakes will be eaten like it was the Last Supper. Once every last one is done, Babe and I clean up the kitchen and put the griddle and mixer away—where they will wait in that cabinet until next Sunday, ready to be used again. This recipe is for small, light, tender pancakes with oh, such a good taste!"

Butter to grease griddle

4 large eggs, separated

2 cups all-purpose flour, sifted

2 teaspoons baking powder

1/2 teaspoon salt

2 tablespoons sugar

6 tablespoons melted butter

2 cups milk (whole or 2 percent)

1 Grease a griddle and preheat over medium-high heat.

2 Place the egg yolks, flour, baking powder, salt, sugar, butter, and milk in a large bowl and beat with a mixer until well blended.

3 In a separate bowl, beat the egg whites until stiff but not dry. Fold the beaten egg whites into the batter.

4 Ladle 1 tablespoon of batter at a time onto the hot griddle. Turn when the surface is dry. These are just as good Monday through Saturday!

MAKES 4 TO 5 SERVINGS.

NOTE: *To keep pancakes warm while cooking the rest, preheat the oven to 200 degrees. Line a cookie sheet with a paper towel and place the pancakes in a single layer. (Avoid stacking them or they can stick or become soggy.) Hold in the oven for up to 10 minutes. Serve immediately as soon as the last batch is cooked.*

YESTERDAY'S GRITS FOR BREAKFAST ✕ ✕

TAMMY ALGOOD (Nashville, Tennessee) called her grandmother Mama, and together they'd sit in aluminum-framed woven plastic chairs on the back porch, where they would talk while shelling peas or snapping beans. Mama, LUCILLE WINDHAM CUMMINGS (Ecru, Mississippi), always had homemade sugar cookies in her cookie jar that looked like a ceramic woven basket with lemons as the lid. Tammy has that cookie jar today, and it makes her smile just seeing it. "Mama's calm attitude and grounded spirit helped show me how Southern women behaved. Love oozed from her, and I always knew she adored me no matter what. Spending the night with her on a Saturday was always such a treat—our ritual included watching *The Lawrence Welk Show*. I thought life couldn't get better than that," says Tammy. "This recipe was how my mama used leftover grits, because no food was ever thrown away. We enjoyed them for breakfast, usually after a big feast the day prior."

Vegetable oil or lard for frying	2 cups leftover grits, cold	1/2 cup all-purpose flour

1 In a large cast-iron skillet over medium heat, heat the grease to a depth of 1/4 inch.
2 Meanwhile, press the cold grits down and cut into 1/2-inch slices. Coat both sides with flour. Test the grease to see if it is hot enough by dropping a drop of water into the grease—it will sizzle when hot enough. Fry the coated slices on one side until golden brown, around 2 minutes. Turn and fry the other side until golden brown. Drain on paper towels and serve warm.

MAKES 6 SERVINGS.

✕✕ BIG MAMA'S BRUNCH CASSEROLE

Unlike many women of her day, VICTORIA POWELL HOPPER (Memphis, Tennessee) was very independent. After the death of Daddy Joe, who was a homebody, she blossomed, traveling and being more social and involved than ever, remembers granddaughter SHEILA SMITH THOMAS (Collierville, Tennessee). Victoria was known as Big Mama to her five grandchildren. Sheila has fond memories of celebrating Christmas Eve at Big Mama and Daddy Joe's house with a tradition of the same wonderful meal—roasted turkey, dressing, her "famous" ambrosia, squash casserole, green beans, and of course, Big Mama's rolls. "The grandkids were never hungry by dinnertime, though, because we were full from all the cookies and candies laid out around the house on the holiday tableware handmade by Big Mama at one of her club meetings. I still have her small holiday plates shaped like snowmen, Santa, and holly leaves that I put out during the holidays. As I remember it now, Big Mama's divinity was always perfect, her pralines so sweet and creamy, and her Mississippi mud cake was about three inches thick, with a fudge and marshmallow topping that I have yet to get close to re-creating. This casserole was served at many bridge-playing brunches with hot fruit compote and Big Mama's infamous melt-in-your-mouth rolls," Sheila says.

6 large eggs, lightly beaten

2 2/3 cups light whipping cream

1 tablespoon brown sugar

1/4 teaspoon paprika

1 tablespoon minced onion

1/2 teaspoon dry mustard

1/2 teaspoon salt

1/2 teaspoon Worcestershire sauce

1/8 teaspoon black pepper

1/8 teaspoon red pepper

Vegetable shortening to prepare dish

8 slices bread, crusts removed

2 pounds sausage, 1 mild and 1 hot, cooked and drained

2 cups shredded sharp Cheddar cheese, divided

1 In a large bowl, combine the eggs, cream, brown sugar, paprika, onion, mustard, salt, Worcestershire sauce, black pepper, and red pepper. Stir well to combine.

2 Grease a 3-quart casserole dish with the shortening and layer with the bread, sausage, and then 1 1/2 cups of the cheese. Cover with the egg mixture. Top with the remaining cheese. Cover and refrigerate overnight.

3 Take out of the refrigerator 2 hours prior to baking. Preheat the oven to 350 degrees. Place the casserole in the oven and bake for 1 hour. Remove from the oven and let sit 20 minutes before serving.

MAKES 8 SERVINGS.

TOMATO BREAKFAST GRAVY ✕ ✕✕

FRANCES W. SMITH was born, raised, and lived all her life in Mount Juliet, Tennessee. Granddaughter BETHANY SMITH TATE (Hendersonville, Tennessee) shares that her family is all about tradition—in fact, they are still honoring one Christmas tradition that has been in her dad's family since the early 1900s. "On Christmas morning it was tradition for my father to go to his grandmother's home like it was tradition for his mother to go to her grandmother's house for a legendary breakfast of tomato gravy and biscuits, sausage, eggs, blackberry and strawberry jams, and her famous Tennessee tea cakes."

1 tablespoon vegetable oil	2 tablespoons all-purpose flour	1/2 cup water
6 sausage patties	1/2 cup tomato juice	Salt and black pepper to taste

1 Grease a large cast-iron skillet with the oil and preheat on medium.
2 Place the sausage patties in the skillet. Cover and cook 5 to 7 minutes. Turn the patties over and continue cooking another 5 to 7 minutes or until the juices run clear. Remove the patties from the skillet, blot on paper towels, and set aside to serve with breakfast.
3 Add the flour to the sausage drippings in the pan and continue stirring until it browns lightly. Add the tomato juice and water a little bit at a time to the hot brown flour. Stirring constantly, cook until it becomes as thick as you desire, approximately 5 minutes. (Do not overcook.) Add salt and pepper to taste. Serve over sausage and hot biscuits for breakfast.

MAKES 4 TO 6 SERVINGS.

SPECIAL-OCCASION FRENCH TOAST

"No matter who was around, my Mamaw always called her husband Mr. William. I never heard her refer to him any other way, and it was beautifully respectful and loving the way she said it," remembers GALE TAYLOR (Starkville, Mississippi). Mamaw was BELL CUMMINGS (Ecru, Mississippi). Mamaw was always happy even though she was in a wheelchair. "I'm in a wheelchair now, and I will forever think of her and how she never let that get her down or influence her feelings negatively. I think it was meant for me to see her daily joy even in the face of what others would consider horrible. It helps me every day to be happy to be alive and enjoy life from a different vantage point," Gale adds. "Every time I would walk in the door, my Mamaw would pinch me on the cheek and say, 'You're my sweetie!' It was so precious to me. And Christmas mornings at Mamaw's—the table legs would all but bend under the weight of that food. She'd prepare every single kind of meat you can imagine, and each had its own gravy. There would also be hot biscuits, jams, jellies, honey—feasts like no others I have ever known," shares Gale.

Vegetable shortening to grease griddle

4 large eggs

1 cup milk (whole or 2 percent)

1 tablespoon honey

½ teaspoon ground cinnamon

12 slices bread

Unsalted butter

Maple syrup

---

1 Grease a griddle and preheat over low to medium heat.
2 In a medium bowl, whisk the eggs until well blended. Add the milk, honey, and cinnamon.
3 Dip the bread slices in the egg mixture and place on the hot griddle. Cook approximately 2 minutes or until golden brown. Flip over and cook approximately 2 minutes longer or until golden brown. Transfer to a serving plate and spread with butter. Keep warm while you continue with the remaining bread slices. Serve warm with maple syrup.

MAKES 6 SERVINGS.

NINETEENTH-CENTURY SPICE MUFFINS

CLARA MAY BENEDICT (Nashville, Tennessee) shares that her paternal grandmother, CAROLINE BENEDICT, moved to Tennessee from New York in the 1880s when one of her brothers opened a lumber mill in Nashville. The youngest of sixteen grandchildren, by the time Clara May was born, her grandmother was in her seventies. She remembers Grandmother as a spry little woman who spent much of her later years sitting in a chair, reading a book, with a cat curled up on her lap. The Benedict family centered around Grandmother, with everyone especially enjoying time spent sitting and talking with her. She was a smart woman with good advice the family respected. She made these muffins quite often, giving the recipe to Clara May's mother, who shared it with her.

Cooking spray

1 1/2 cups sugar

2/3 cups vegetable shortening

2 large eggs, beaten

2 cups all-purpose flour

1/2 teaspoon salt

1 teaspoon baking soda

1 teaspoon ground cinnamon

1/2 teaspoon nutmeg

1/2 teaspoon ground cloves

1 cup buttermilk

Powdered sugar (optional)

1 Preheat the oven to 350 degrees. Spray 18 muffin tin cups with cooking spray or use baking cups.

2 In a large bowl cream together the sugar and shortening. Add the eggs. In a sifter, combine the flour, salt, baking soda, cinnamon, nutmeg, and cloves. Sift and add to the bowl alternately with the buttermilk. Mix well. Pour into the muffin tins, filling the cups one-third full. (Do not overfill, as they will bubble over.)

3 Bake for 20 to 25 minutes or until a toothpick inserted in the center comes out clean. Cool on a wire rack before removing from the tins. Serve plain or sprinkle with powdered sugar before serving.

MAKES APPROXIMATELY 18 MUFFINS.

JULES'S BLUEBERRY SAUSAGE CASSEROLE

Grandma Jules is what siblings JACKSON CAMPBELL and KATHERINE PAIGE HELTSLEY (Nashville, Tennessee) call JULIE EATON HELTSLEY (Tullahoma, Tennessee). Jackson and Katherine enjoy spending time at their Grandma Jules's house, especially on holidays and for special weekend sleepovers. And everyone knows that summer is the best time to visit, when the garden's coming in and the blueberries are ripe! Jules uses an acre and a half of their twenty-seven-acre farm to grow fruits and vegetables, which she cans or freezes so the family can enjoy them year-round. When the grandkids help her pick, they enjoy eating just as many berries as they pick. But if there happen to be any left in the basket, Jules uses the fresh berries to make all kinds of tasty treats—including this breakfast casserole. Jackson and Katherine say they love it because they get to have two of their favorite things for breakfast—blueberries and cake!

CASSEROLE:

1/2 cup (1 stick) butter, softened

3/4 cup sugar

1/4 cup brown sugar

2 large eggs

2 cups all-purpose flour

1 teaspoon baking powder

1/2 teaspoon baking soda

1 (8 ounce) container sour cream

1 pound sausage, cooked and drained

1 cup blueberries, fresh or frozen

1/2 cup chopped pecans

SAUCE:

1/2 cup sugar

2 tablespoons cornstarch

1/2 cup water

2 cups blueberries

1/2 teaspoon lemon juice

1 Preheat the oven to 350 degrees.

2 TO MAKE THE CASSEROLE, in a large bowl beat the butter. Add the sugar and brown sugar and beat until mixed well. Add the eggs, one at a time, beating one minute after each addition.

3 In a medium bowl combine the flour, baking powder, and baking soda. Add the flour mixture and sour cream alternately into the butter mixture. Beat after each addition. Fold in the sausage and blueberries.

4 Pour into an ungreased 9 x 13-inch casserole dish. Spread the batter evenly and sprinkle with pecans. (To make ahead, you can cover and refrigerate overnight or until you are ready to bake.) Bake for 35 to 40 minutes or until the cake tests done.

5 **TO MAKE THE SAUCE,** In a medium glass bowl, combine the sugar and cornstarch. Add the water and blueberries. Cook on medium-high for 1 minute in the microwave. Stir and continue cooking until thickened. Remove from the microwave and stir in the lemon juice. Serve alongside the warm casserole or spoon it over individual portions.

MAKES 9 TO 12 SERVINGS.

BREAKFAST CHEESE BREAD

SANDRA MEADOWS (Nashville, Tennessee) was born in Murfreesboro, Tennessee. She is known as Nini to her four grandchildren—two boys and two girls—all of whom live in Tennessee. According to granddaughter AVA MEADOWS (Brentwood, Tennessee), "Nini decorates her house for every holiday, and she always lets me and my cousins help. She is a wonderful grandmother, and we all adore her." Nini shares that she loves this recipe because it's quick and easy and always a hit with the grandchildren. It's great to eat for breakfast or any other time of the day.

Cooking spray

2 ²/₃ cups baking mix

3/4 cup whole milk

2 large eggs, lightly beaten

2 teaspoons dry mustard

1 ¹/₂ cups shredded sharp Cheddar cheese, divided

2 tablespoons butter

1 Preheat the oven to 350 degrees. Lightly spray a large loaf pan.

2 In a large bowl stir the baking mix and milk with a spoon. Add the eggs, mustard, and 1 cup of the cheese. Pour into the loaf pan. Sprinkle the remaining cheese on top and dot with butter.

3 Bake 45 to 50 minutes. Cool in the pan for 10 minutes, and then remove and cool on a wire rack before slicing.

MAKES 10 TO 12 SERVINGS.

NANA'S SAUSAGE CHEESE BITES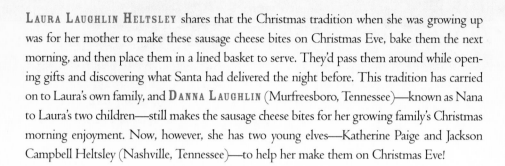

LAURA LAUGHLIN HELTSLEY shares that the Christmas tradition when she was growing up was for her mother to make these sausage cheese bites on Christmas Eve, bake them the next morning, and then place them in a lined basket to serve. They'd pass them around while opening gifts and discovering what Santa had delivered the night before. This tradition has carried on to Laura's own family, and DANNA LAUGHLIN (Murfreesboro, Tennessee)—known as Nana to Laura's two children—still makes the sausage cheese bites for her growing family's Christmas morning enjoyment. Now, however, she has two young elves—Katherine Paige and Jackson Campbell Heltsley (Nashville, Tennessee)—to help her make them on Christmas Eve!

---

1 pound ground sausage, uncooked, at room temperature

3 cups biscuit mix

4 cups shredded sharp Cheddar cheese

Cooking spray

---

1 In a large bowl mix together the raw sausage and biscuit mix, using your hands. Add the cheese and mix until evenly distributed. The mixture will be crumbly.

2 Using your hands, roll the mixture into bite-size balls, squeezing so the mixture holds together. (If the mixture is too dry, try adding a few drops of water.) At this point you can either bake them or freeze until ready to serve. (Nana freezes hers overnight and bakes them the next morning—she swears it makes all the difference!)

3 When ready to bake, preheat the oven to 375 degrees. Spray a large cookie sheet with cooking spray. Place the balls on the cookie sheet approximately 1 inch apart. Bake for 9 to 10 minutes; then turn over to prevent sticking. Bake an additional 9 to 10 minutes or until golden brown. Remove from the cookie sheet and serve warm or at room temperature.

MAKES 3 DOZEN BALLS.

NOTE: *It's important not to precook the sausage before mixing with the other ingredients. Working with the raw sausage at room temperature is best, and it's imperative to mix the ingredients very well or the mixture won't stick together. To bake from frozen, thaw on the cookie sheet 15 minutes before baking.*

✕✕✕ TORI'S QUICHE

SHEILA SMITH THOMAS (Collierville, Tennessee) was the first grandchild for VICTORIA "TORI" POWELL HOPPER (Memphis, Tennessee). As new grandparents, Victoria hoped to be called Mama Vicki and her husband, Big Daddy. However, as is common with little ones learning to speak, Shelia had her own idea of what her grandparents would be called, and ignored the many attempts to correct her. Shelia's grandparents became lovingly known as Big Mama and Daddy Joe—first by her . . . and then by all five grandchildren. Sheila says Big Mama was very active in the community—holding positions in her garden, book, and Presbyterian Women's clubs, playing bridge, and dancing weekly at the senior center. She worked outside the home in administrative positions for the City of Memphis offices when many women did not. She truly represented the woman in the 1970s commercial, as she could "'bring home the bacon and fry it up in a pan'—she really did do it all, and did it well. As with so many families, Big Mama was the glue that kept our family together. We all really miss her—she passed away in 1989 at the age of seventy."

4 to 5 slices bacon*

1/2 cup chopped onion

1/4 cup chopped green bell pepper

1 (4 ounce) can mushrooms (optional)

1 (9 inch) frozen piecrust

4 ounces Cheddar cheese, sliced

3/4 cup nonfat milk

2 large eggs

Dash of cayenne pepper

Salt to taste

Dash of nutmeg

1 Preheat the oven to 450 degrees.
2 Cook the bacon until crisp. Remove and drain on paper towels, reserving the bacon drippings. Sauté the onion, pepper, and mushrooms in the bacon drippings. Drain. Place in the unbaked piecrust and add a single layer of cheese.
3 In a small bowl combine the milk, eggs, cayenne pepper, salt, and nutmeg and pour evenly over the cheese.
4 Bake for 12 minutes, reduce the temperature to 325 degrees, and continue baking for 25 to 30 minutes or until the egg mixture is set. Slice and serve warm.

MAKES 8 SERVINGS.

* You can substitute cooked sausage or ham for the bacon.

JULESY'S "BLOOB-BERRY" BREAKFAST MUFFINS ✕ ✕ ✕

Jules or Julesy is what brothers MacLaine and Grayson Butters (Brentwood, Tennessee) and the other grandchildren call Julie Eaton Heltsley (Tullahoma, Tennessee). MacLaine and Grayson love to visit Grandpa and Jules on their little farm in the country. When they are not busy playing with Jazz the cat or swinging high on the tire swing, the boys love to "help" Jules pick blueberries from her six huge bushes, using the "pick-one-eat-one" method. When MacLaine was a toddler, he coined the term "bloob-berries" to describe the tasty treats on those bushes. These light and easy blueberry muffins are a favorite of everyone in the family, especially on Sunday mornings before church. Uncles and growing grandkids all get a kick out of stacking their used muffin cups to compare how many they ate (not that anyone's counting, of course).

Cooking spray

1 large egg

1/2 cup whole milk

1/4 cup canola oil

1/2 teaspoon vanilla extract

1 1/2 cups all-purpose flour

1/2 cup sugar, plus a pinch for the top of each muffin

2 teaspoons baking powder

1/2 teaspoon salt

1 cup fresh or frozen blueberries*

---

1 Preheat the oven to 400 degrees. Spray 12 muffin tin cups with cooking spray or use baking cups.

2 In a large bowl beat the egg. Whisk in the milk, oil, and vanilla. Add the flour, sugar, baking powder, and salt, and mix until the flour is moistened. (The batter should be a little lumpy.) Gently stir in the blueberries.

3 Fill the muffin cups two-thirds full. Sprinkle a little sugar on top. Bake 20 to 25 minutes or until lightly brown on top. Serve warm or at room temperature.

MAKES 1 DOZEN MUFFINS.

* Frozen berries, straight from the freezer, work best. Fresh ones may turn your batter an unappetizing purple color.

GRANNY'S FRUIT COMPOTE ✕ ✕ ✕

MARK HINTON (Hermitage, Tennessee) recalls being at his grandparents' house nearly every weekend when he was growing up. LYDA WINFREY (Lascassas, Tennessee) grew most of her own produce, so Mark remembers her as always cooking. Lyda was known to her five grandsons as Granny. Mark can still see the big old stove in her kitchen. It had a burner built inside the stove where, through the top, they'd place a large pot on it to cook the beans or other vegetables they had grown. Because he spent so much time around Granny in the kitchen, Mark says he's picked up on how she did things and has been able to apply that to his own cooking.

Cooking spray

1 (20 ounce) can pineapple chunks

1 (15 ounce) can apricots

1 (15 ounce) can sliced pears

1 (29 ounce) can sliced peaches

1 small (12 ounce) jar cherries

½ cup (1 stick) butter

1 cup sugar

1 cup brown sugar

2 cinnamon sticks

½ teaspoon nutmeg

1 Preheat the oven to 325 degrees. Lightly spray a 9 x 13-inch baking pan.

2 Drain all of the fruit and mix together in a large bowl. Pour into the baking pan.

3 In a medium saucepan melt the butter. Mix in the sugar, brown sugar, cinnamon sticks, and nutmeg. Stirring constantly, bring the mixture to a boil and remove from the heat. Pour the mixture over the fruit.

4 Bake for 25 to 30 minutes or until bubbly. Serve warm on biscuits, as a complement to an egg casserole for brunch, as a topping on pound cake, or over your favorite ice cream for dessert. Remove the cinnamon sticks before serving.

MAKES 10 TO 12 SERVINGS.

"SWEET AS CAN BE" CARAMEL PECAN ROLLS

Grandson **CHARLIE PERKINS** (Nashville, Tennessee) shares that his grandma **ALICE "SISSY" TARUMIANZ** (Lookout Mountain, Tennessee) gives really great hugs. She is known as Sissy to family and friends and as Sis-Sis to her six grandchildren. Charlie loves playing outside with her, going to the park, and pretending to fix things with all of her tools. And like any loving grandma, Sis-Sis has been known to be the best at fixing boo-boos with her sweet kisses, Band-Aids, and the occasional Popsicle. Sis-Sis is a great cook and baker and taught Charlie's mom, Laura Perkins, her way around the kitchen. Charlie is already proving to be a good helper to his mom and Sis-Sis.

TOPPING:

5 tablespoons butter

3/4 cup brown sugar

1/4 cup water

1/2 cup chopped pecans

ROLLS:

2 (8 ounce) cans crescent rolls

3 tablespoons butter, softened

1/2 cup sugar

2 teaspoons ground cinnamon

1 Preheat the oven to 375 degrees.

2 TO MAKE THE TOPPING, in a 9 x 13-inch baking pan, melt the butter. Stir in the brown sugar, water, and pecans.

3 TO MAKE THE ROLLS, separate each can of crescent roll dough into four rectangles and seal perforations. Spread with the softened butter. In a small bowl combine the sugar and cinnamon and sprinkle over the buttered dough.

4 Roll up each rectangle from the short side. Cut each roll into four slices. Place in the prepared pan, cut side down on top of the brown sugar, butter, and pecan mixture.

5 Bake for 20 to 25 minutes until lightly browned. Invert immediately and spoon any remaining sauce over the tops of the rolls. Serve warm for breakfast. Sis-Sis says these freeze beautifully!

MAKES 16 SERVINGS.

GRANDMA'S BUTTERMILK WAFFLES ✕ ✕ ✕

"Gimme some sugar" is what Grandma BETTY KING (Candler, North Carolina) would request of granddaughter MEGAN KING HOOPINGARNER (Murfreesboro, Tennessee) when she wanted a little kiss. Megan remembers many summers visiting her grandma and grandpa in North Carolina, where she would always help with cooking and baking. One summer Grandma taught her how to make homemade buttermilk biscuits, and Megan says she was elbows deep in dough in no time! "Grandma still brags to this day that I was and still am the best buttermilk adder of all time. It's a very special memory for both of us. I can also remember the first time I saw my grandma without her teeth. She took them out and told me if I didn't brush my teeth every day that I would end up like her, with dentures. Scared me half to death," Megan adds. This recipe was created by Megan's great-grandma and perfected by Grandma King.

2 cups sifted all-purpose flour	1 teaspoon baking soda	2 large eggs
1 teaspoon salt	3 tablespoons vegetable shortening	2 cups buttermilk
1 teaspoon baking powder		Cooking spray

1 In a large bowl mix together the flour, salt, baking powder, and baking soda. Cut in the shortening and add the eggs and buttermilk. Mix well.

2 Preheat the waffle iron and spray with cooking spray. Ladle the batter onto the hot waffle iron, and cook until golden brown, approximately 3 1/2 minutes or according to the directions on your waffle maker.

3 Keep warm in a 200-degree oven until all the waffles are cooked. Serve warm with your favorite syrup, fruit, nut, or whipped topping for breakfast, or for dinner with Chicken and Doop on page 148.

MAKES 4 TO 6 SERVINGS.

OLD-FASHIONED DOUGHNUTS

EVELYN HINTON (Hermitage, Tennessee) was born in Jordonia, Tennessee. Grandson GARRETT HINTON (also of Hermitage) has fond memories of spending the night at her house. Known to her grandchildren as Mimi, Evelyn was one to make sure the grandkids had a special bedtime snack anytime they slept over because she didn't want them to go to bed hungry! As a little one, Garrett remembers her sitting him on the counter (just as she did with his older sister and cousins) so he could help her stir the batter for muffins or pancakes. Mimi passed away in 2007, but Garrett's special memories are never far from his mind—he and his family now live in Mimi's house. Mimi was taught the doughnut recipe from her father-in-law, John Hinton.

---

4 cups all-purpose flour, plus extra for rolling out dough

4 teaspoons baking powder

1/2 teaspoon salt

1 cup sugar

2 tablespoons butter, melted

2 large eggs, beaten

1 cup whole milk

1 tablespoon nutmeg

Lard or vegetable shortening for frying

Cinnamon sugar (optional)

Strawberry or chocolate icing (optional)

Sprinkles (optional)

---

1 In a large bowl add the flour, baking powder, salt, sugar, butter, eggs, milk, and nutmeg. Stir until the flour mixture is moistened, but not much more.

2 Roll the dough to 1/2 inch thick on a floured surface and let stand for 15 to 18 minutes. Cut the dough with a floured 2 1/2- or 3-inch doughnut or biscuit cutter.

3 In a deep skillet or fryer, heat 1 1/2 inches of lard or shortening to 370 degrees, keeping the temperature as steady as possible. Fry the doughnuts and turn using a wooden spoon when the first crack appears. Continue cooking until browned nicely, about 45 to 50 seconds per side.

3 Remove from the grease and drain on paper towels or brown paper to absorb excess grease. Eat plain or sprinkle with cinnamon sugar. Or for the grandkids, add strawberry or chocolate icing and sprinkles.

MAKES ABOUT 2 DOZEN DOUGHNUTS.

GRANDMOTHER CALDWELL'S PETITE COFFEE CAKES ✕ ✕ ✕

Mrs. R. W. "Ethel" Caldwell (Lawrenceburg, Tennessee) was known to her grandkids as Grandmother or Mrs. Caldwell. She was a dignified, true Southern lady to whom manners were paramount—that's why grandson Brian Carden (Nashville, Tennessee) says he only called her Granny once. He recalls, "Grandmother and Granddaddy's house was at the end of a long, tree-lined street, and as soon as we made the turn, I could see the driveway and the garage. Dad always had to slow to a crawl to keep the car from scraping, but I remember the anticipation of getting there. My sense of smell recalls so many fond memories of those days—Granddaddy's Old Spice aftershave . . . the smell of the house . . . the kitchen . . . the garage . . . whatever was baking in the kitchen. My mom said Grandmother never used a true recipe, just a dash of this and a little of that. No matter how she made it, it always was perfect in our eyes. When I graduated college and moved from Knoxville to Nashville, Mom made me a recipe book, and these coffee cakes are one of Grandmother's best."

PETITE CAKES:
Cooking spray

1/2 cup (1 stick) margarine, softened

1 cup sugar

2 large eggs

2 cups all-purpose flour, sifted

1 teaspoon baking soda

1 teaspoon baking powder

1 teaspoon salt

1 teaspoon vanilla extract

TOPPING:
1/2 cup brown sugar

1/4 cup sugar

2 teaspoons ground cinnamon

1 cup pecans, crushed

1 Preheat the oven to 350 degrees. Lightly grease 2 muffin tins with cooking spray.

2 **To make the petite cakes**, in a large bowl cream together the margarine and sugar. Add the eggs and blend well. Add the flour, then the baking soda, baking powder, salt, and vanilla.

3 Mix well and pour into 24 muffin cups, filling one-half full.

4 **To make the topping**, combine the brown sugar, sugar, and cinnamon. Sprinkle on top of the muffins before baking. Then sprinkle with the crushed pecans. Bake for 30 minutes or until the center tests done with a toothpick.

MAKES 24 MUFFINS.

Skillet Biscuits

Spoon Rolls

Banana Butterscotch Bread

Pumpkin Bread

Nanny's Buttermilk Cornbread

Grandma Littrell's Parker House Rolls

Chocolate Chip Muffins

No-Knead Yeast Bread

Old Mommie Bread (a.k.a. Cinnamon Rolls)

Granny's Yeast Rolls

Sweet Potato Biscuits

Granny Pearl's Homemade Rolls

Mamie's Overnight Rolls

Vallie's From-Scratch Banana Bread

Breads, Rolls, and Biscuits

✕✕✕ SKILLET BISCUITS

LARISSA ARNAULT (Nashville, Tennessee) shares that her mother was a Yankee who married into a quintessential Mississippi family, and goulash would not do for her daddy. So Mamaw Lucy, LUCY HARRIS (Weir, Mississippi), "took my mom under her wing and taught her all the Southern fundamentals—biscuits, lemon ice box pie, fried chicken. My parents and I moved away from Mississippi, but my mother has since taught those recipes to me, and I think of Mamaw Lucy each time I make them," Larissa says.

---

2 heaping cups self-rising flour, plus extra for rolling out dough

½ cup buttermilk, divided

2 tablespoons vegetable oil, divided

Oil to grease the skillet

---

1 Preheat the oven to 400 degrees.

2 In a medium bowl add the flour. Pour ¹/4 cup of the buttermilk into the flour. Add 1 tablespoon of the oil directly into the buttermilk. (Do not pour the oil directly on the flour.) Mix until heavy and slightly sticky, adding additional buttermilk and oil as needed.

3 Dust a linen kitchen towel with flour and lay on the counter. Place dough on the floured towel and knead lightly two to three times. Do not over-knead. The texture should be slightly crumbly but still able to mush together.

4 Roll out the dough with a floured rolling pin to about 1-inch thickness. Cut biscuits with a small glass or with a 2-inch cutter.

5 Pour a thin layer of oil into a cast-iron skillet. Dab each biscuit in oil and flip, placing into the skillet. Biscuits will be touching each other in the skillet. Let the biscuits rise in the skillet on top of the stove for 2 minutes.

6 Bake 20 to 25 minutes until the bottoms are golden brown.

MAKES 10 TO 12 BISCUITS.

ARLENE RAINES (Goodlettsville, Tennessee) shares that her Nana, ELLEN OGLESBY MAYS (Asheville, North Carolina), was quite the lady. Even well into her nineties she dressed every morning and kept her hands well manicured and nails polished and her hair coiffed and lipstick fresh. She didn't get to see Nana often because she lived hundreds of miles away, but when she did visit, they always went on adventures in the beautiful mountains of North Carolina and shopping excursions downtown. Nana was quite accomplished on the piano and composed many pieces of music. Arlene remembers when she was ten, she spent a month with her, learning to play the piano, and Nana purchased the family's first practice piano. Nana was committed to healthful living, was always trying new recipes, and wasn't afraid to be adventuresome with food.

4 cups self-rising flour	1 package dry yeast	3/4 cup vegetable shortening
2 cups lukewarm water	1 large egg	Cooking spray
	1/4 cup sugar	

1 In a large bowl add the flour, water, yeast, egg, sugar, and shortening, and mix well. Cover and refrigerate until ready to bake. You do not need to wait for the rolls to rise. (This batter will keep for several days covered in the refrigerator.)

2 When ready to bake, preheat the oven to 400 degrees. Lightly spray 24 muffin tin cups and spoon the batter into the muffin tins, filling each cup one-half full with batter. Bake for 15 minutes or until golden brown.

MAKES APPROXIMATELY 24 ROLLS.

✕✕✕ BANANA BUTTERSCOTCH BREAD

When Sueanne Kyle (from Martinsville, Virginia) or any of the other grandchildren went to Nanny's house, they'd walk in and holler for her. Nanny, Virginia Kester (also of Martinsville, Virginia), would always holler back "woo-hoo" to let them know where she was in the house. Sueanne also shares that whenever she was heading back to college at Virginia Tech, she'd stop in and have lunch with Nanny. Right before she'd leave, Nanny would hand her a $20 bill saying, "You always need to have some mad money in your pocket!" (Sueanne now lives in Marlborough, Massachusetts.)

Vegetable shortening and flour to prepare pan

1 3/4 cups all-purpose flour

2 teaspoons baking powder

1/2 teaspoon baking soda

1/2 teaspoon salt

1/2 teaspoon ground cinnamon

1/2 teaspoon nutmeg

2 mashed ripe bananas

3/4 cup sugar

2 large eggs

1/4 cup melted butter

1/4 cup whole milk

1 (6 ounce) package butterscotch chips

1 cup roasted pecans, chopped

---

1 Preheat the oven to 350 degrees. Grease and flour a large loaf pan.

2 In a large bowl combine the flour, baking powder, baking soda, salt, ground cinnamon, and nutmeg.

3 In a small bowl combine the bananas, sugar, eggs, and melted butter.

4 Alternately add the banana mixture and milk to the flour mixture—beating well after each addition. Stir in the butterscotch chips and nuts. Pour the batter into the loaf pan.

5 Bake for about 45 minutes or until a toothpick inserted in the center comes out clean. Let cool in the pan for 20 minutes; then put on a wire rack to cool completely. Serve warm or at room temperature. Wrap with plastic wrap or put into a big zip-top bag and store in the refrigerator.

MAKES 1 LOAF.

PUMPKIN BREAD ✕✕✕

LYNNE LOUISE NIELSEN BROWN (Duluth, Georgia) was born in Pittsburgh, Pennsylvania. She is known to grandson TOBIN ORENDORF (Marietta, Georgia) as Grammy. Tobin's mom, Christie Brown Orendorf, remembers Grammy growing lots of tomatoes in her garden each year and canning the tomatoes for sauce. Christie shares that every year Grammy baked this pumpkin bread as thank-you gifts for her and her brothers' teachers. Tobin's mom bakes a lot now, having learned from her mom (Grammy) and her Grandma Nielsen. This pumpkin bread is a treasured family favorite.

Vegetable shortening

3 cups sugar

1 cup corn or canola oil

4 large eggs

3 1/2 cups all-purpose flour

1 teaspoon baking powder

2 teaspoons baking soda

2 teaspoons salt

2 teaspoons ground cinnamon

1 teaspoon nutmeg

1 teaspoon allspice

2/3 cup water

1 (15 ounce) can pumpkin (100 percent pure pumpkin)

1 cup chopped walnuts

1 Preheat the oven to 350 degrees. Grease (not flour) 2 large or 4 small bread pans.
2 Mix the sugar, oil, and eggs together in a large bowl with an electric mixer until well blended.
3 In a separate large bowl, add the flour, baking powder, baking soda, salt, cinnamon, nutmeg, and allspice. Blend the dry mixture into the wet mixture, a little at a time. Add the water, pumpkin, and walnuts.
4 Pour the batter into the bread pans and bake for 55 to 60 minutes or until a toothpick inserted in the center comes out clean.
5 Set the bread pans on a cooling rack to cool for approximately 20 minutes. Remove the bread from the pans and slice. Serve alone or with butter or cream cheese.

MAKES 2 LARGE LOAVES OR 4 SMALL ONES.

NANNY'S BUTTERMILK CORNBREAD

"This is the most important recipe I have of my grandmother's," shares granddaughter DEBORAH S. EBERMAN (Gulf Breeze, Florida). "This one food touches my heart when I think of my grandmother and touches my soul when I think of our huge family sitting around her table, sharing a meal together. Each time we ate it, someone would declare that it was the best she'd ever made," Deborah recalls. Her most precious memories—holiday dressing, cold winter days with soup, or summer days with wilted lettuce—all involve this recipe. Her grandmother was CLARA LILLIAN VERNON WADE (Fort Smith, Arkansas).

---

3 tablespoons vegetable shortening or bacon drippings

2 1/2 cups cornmeal

I cup all-purpose flour

3 heaping teaspoons baking powder

1/2 teaspoon baking soda

2 teaspoons salt

2 teaspoons sugar

2 1/2 cups buttermilk

2 large eggs

---

1 Preheat the oven to 500 degrees.

2 Put the shortening in a 9 x 11-inch pan and place in the oven to warm while you mix the cornbread.

3 In a large bowl mix the cornmeal, flour, baking powder, soda, salt, and sugar together with a wooden spoon. Add the buttermilk and stir.

4 Remove the melted shortening from the oven and pour into the cornmeal mixture. Add the eggs and mix again with a wooden spoon.

5 Pour the batter into the warm pan and bake for approximately 25 minutes or until the center tests done with a toothpick.

MAKES 8 TO 10 SERVINGS.

NOTE: *For the perfect cornbread, it's important to use a wooden spoon and not to overmix. Once you combine dry and wet ingredients, you want to mix enough to moisten but not too much, or the finished bread may turn out tough or dry.*

GRANDMA LITTRELL'S PARKER HOUSE ROLLS ✕✕✕

TAMMY GIBSON (Springfield, Tennessee) shares that her grandma, FANNIE PEARL FUGETT LITTRELL (Mendon, Missouri), "was such a gentle soul and cornerstone in our lives. She never judged us and was always there to encourage us. We were very fortunate to have our grandparents so close to us. We lived on a farm outside of town, and my grandparents lived in town. Every day my grandparents would come out to the farm to spend the day working, canning, gardening, etc. I never saw my grandmother measure anything for a recipe; it was always a pinch of this, a dash of that, a smidgen of that. It really made it hard to replicate! I was very young when I first got to help Grandma cut these rolls and smother them in butter—what a mess we made! I remember having to stand on a chair to even reach the table, but Grandma always let us help."

---

3 to 4 cups all-purpose flour, sifted, plus extra for rolling out dough

Pinch of salt

2 to 3 tablespoons sugar

1 package yeast, dissolved

1 large egg, beaten

3 tablespoons vegetable shortening

Melted butter to brush tops

---

1 Measure 3 cups of the flour into a large bowl. Add the salt and blend thoroughly.
2 Dissolve the sugar in the yeast and add the beaten egg; then combine with the flour mixture.
3 Add the shortening and knead into a medium soft, smooth dough, using more of the flour if necessary.
4 Let it rise until doubled in size. Knead it down lightly and let it rise again until doubled in size. Turn the dough onto a lightly floured cutting board.
5 Roll gently into a sheet 1/3 inch thick. Cut with a floured biscuit cutter. (Tammy's grandmother used a water glass.) Brush with melted butter and fold in half. Let rise until very light.
6 Preheat the oven to 375 degrees. Bake 15 to 20 minutes, or less time if your rolls are small.

MAKES 2 TO 3 DOZEN ROLLS, DEPENDING ON SIZE.

CHOCOLATE CHIP MUFFINS ✕✕✕

These muffins are the absolute favorite of **CAL HOLLIS** (Nashville, Tennessee). Cal loves to mix the dry ingredients and shake the cinnamon on top of the muffins. His big sister, **GENTRY ANNE**, is terrific with the whisk, so she helps with the wet ingredients. They enjoy Sunday mornings at their family's mountain house with their parents and Nana, **SUSAN GENTRY WILLIAMS** (also of Nashville). The kids share that Nana's muffins smell wonderful when baking and taste delicious!

MUFFINS:

2 large eggs

2/3 cup whole milk

1 1/2 teaspoons vanilla extract

2 cups all-purpose flour

2/3 cups sugar

2 1/2 teaspoons baking powder

1/4 teaspoon salt

1 cup semisweet chocolate chips

1/2 cup (1 stick) butter, melted and cooled

CINNAMON SUGAR TOPPING:

1 tablespoon sugar

1/2 teaspoon ground cinnamon

1 Preheat the oven to 375 degrees. Line 2 (12-cup) muffin tins with baking cups.

2 **TO MAKE THE MUFFINS**, in a bowl whisk together the eggs, milk, and vanilla.

3 In a large bowl whisk together the flour, sugar, baking powder, and salt. Stir in the chocolate chips.

4 With a rubber spatula or wooden spoon, fold the egg mixture, along with the melted butter, into the flour mixture and stir only until the ingredients are moistened and combined. (Do not overmix or you will have tough muffins.) Evenly fill the muffin cups with the batter, using an ice-cream scoop.

5 **TO MAKE THE TOPPING**, in a small bowl combine the sugar and cinnamon. Sprinkle a little topping on each muffin. (Susan uses an old salt shaker.)

6 Place the muffin tin in the oven and bake for 18 to 20 minutes, or until a toothpick inserted in the center of a muffin comes out clean. Transfer to a wire rack and let cool for 5 to 10 minutes before removing from the pan. These freeze well.

MAKES 2 DOZEN MUFFINS.

NO-KNEAD YEAST BREAD

Arlene Raines (Goodlettsville, Tennessee) shares that her Nana, Ellen Oglesby Mays (Asheville, North Carolina), passed away in 1986 at the age of ninety-seven. Nana was married at eighteen, widowed at twenty-eight, and was left with two young children to raise on her own—a tough task anytime, but especially before the advent of Social Security. She was resourceful, resilient, unafraid to try new things, and very independent. Arlene likes to think that observing Nana's life infused some of those qualities in her, the only granddaughter. "Nana loved to bake whole wheat bread. As she got older, she was unable to knead the bread. She found and adapted a recipe for no-knead whole wheat bread so she could continue to bake fresh bread. It was always a little bit crumbly, but oh so delicious. If she were still alive, she would love today's bread-making machines. I believe her healthful eating contributed to her long life, and she instilled in me a true love for homemade whole wheat bread," Arlene concludes.

I to 2 tablespoons vegetable shortening, plus extra to prepare pan

1 (.25 ounce) package dry yeast

1 1/2 cups warm water

1/3 cup molasses

1/2 teaspoon salt

4 1/2 to 5 cups whole grain flour

1 Grease a loaf pan.
2 In a large bowl mix the yeast in warm water. Add the molasses and let stand for 5 minutes.
3 Stir the shortening, salt, and flour into the yeast mixture. (One learns from practice whether the particular flour being used calls for the larger or smaller amounts of shortening and flour, since all grains are not the same texture.) Do not use an electric mixer.
4 Spoon the bread mixture into the loaf pan, set in a warm place, and let rise until nearly double in size, 45 to 60 minutes.
5 Preheat the oven to 350 degrees and bake for 45 to 50 minutes.

MAKES 1 LOAF.

ARLENE'S NOTE: *One should expect a heavier, coarser texture but more delicious bread when using whole grain flour. Mixtures of whole soy flour in proportion of 1 to 4 with whole wheat flour make a nice bread, but less shortening is required. I prefer a loaf of soy and whole wheat bread started with the oven at 150 degrees and brought up to 350 degrees, then cut back to about 275 degrees to finish the last 15 minutes of baking.*

OLD MOMMIE BREAD (A.K.A. CINNAMON ROLLS)

CAROL ANN RUPP CRAWLEY (Alton, Virginia) is known as Old Mommie to her nine grandchildren, seven of whom were born in the South. (The other two, Maika and Jun Ito, were born and are being raised in Tokyo, Japan.) The newest addition, grandchild number nine, is DANIEL ALEXANDER KIRKPATRICK (Fairfax, Virginia). If he's anything like his cousins, his mom (Kara Crawley Kirkpatrick) predicts that he, too, will look forward to this favorite food item when he visits—Old Mommie's famous cinnamon rolls. Older cousins Wade and Jun like to help make these, rolling the dough, spreading the butter, and adding the brown sugar and cinnamon. Based on how generous these "helpers" are with the ingredients, oftentimes the rolls are extra-sweet or cinnamony, but eaten regardless. Once, two of the grandchildren consumed eighteen rolls in no time flat!

DOUGH STARTER:

2 cups hot water

3 tablespoons instant potatoes

3/4 cup sugar

ROLLS:

1 cup dough starter

2 cups hot water, divided

3 tablespoons instant potatoes

1 1/2 cups plus 2 teaspoons sugar, divided

2 tablespoons yeast

1 cup lukewarm water

1 cup vegetable oil

1 tablespoon salt

2 large eggs

1 bag (5 pounds) bread flour

Vegetable oil to grease mixing bowl

Vegetable shortening to prepare cookie sheet

CINNAMON ROLL FILLING:

5 cups firmly packed brown sugar

1/4 cup and 1 tablespoon ground cinnamon

2 1/2 cups raisins (optional)

2 1/2 cups chopped walnuts or pecans (optional)

2 1/2 cups butter, softened

ICING:

3 cups powdered sugar

1/4 cup (1/2 stick) margarine, softened

1 teaspoon vanilla extract

3 tablespoons whole milk

1 **To make the dough starter**, prepare it a week before you plan on making the rolls. In a glass jar mix the hot water, instant potatoes, and sugar well. Seal the jar and allow to ferment on the counter overnight. Then place in the refrigerator to be used when you are ready to make the rolls.

2 Preheat the oven to 340 degrees.

3 **To make the rolls**, take out 1 cup of the dough starter for the recipe and "feed" the remainder in the jar with 1 cup of the hot water, instant potatoes, and 3/4 cup of the sugar. Do this each time you remove a cup to make these rolls.

4 Dissolve the yeast in the lukewarm water and add 2 teaspoons of the sugar. Mix thoroughly. Set aside and let it get foamy.

5 In a large bowl mix the dough starter, the remaining 1 cup hot water, oil, salt, the remaining 3/4 cup sugar, and eggs. Blend thoroughly and add the foamy yeast mixture. Gradually add the flour until the mixture begins to pull away from the bowl.

6 Place the remainder of the flour in a large bowl and transfer the batter to the bowl, kneading by hand until it no longer sticks to your hands. Remove from the bowl, empty out any remaining flour, grease a large bowl with oil, and place the dough in the bowl, turning it over so all sides are coated with oil.

7 Cover and keep in a draft-free location until double in size. (Carol usually turns on the oven light and places the dough in the oven for rising time. The heat from the light is enough to make dough rise quickly.)

8 **To prepare and add the filling**, in a small bowl combine the brown sugar and cinnamon. Stir in raisins or nuts, if desired.

9 When the dough is double in size, pinch off two large handfuls of dough and roll it out in a rectangular shape. Using a pastry brush, spread the dough evenly with the softened butter, sprinkle generously with the brown sugar mixture, and roll up jelly roll–style.

10 Slice into 1 1/2-inch-thick slices, pinching the seam to seal after slicing. Place the rolls three wide on a 9 x 13-inch greased jelly-roll pan; rolls should not be touching at this point. Using the tines of a fork, poke each roll twice on top to allow air to escape. Allow to rise until double in size, 35 to 40 minutes.

11 Bake for 15 to 20 minutes until lightly browned on top.

12 **To make the icing**, in a medium bowl use a hand mixer to cream together the sugar and margarine. Mix in the vanilla and milk and blend until smooth. Spread the icing over warm rolls and serve.

MAKES APPROXIMATELY 5 DOZEN ROLLS.

GRANNY'S YEAST ROLLS

DOROTHY SUE SULLIVAN has lived all of her life in Lyles, Tennessee. Granddaughter **JENNIFER SULLIVAN BROWN** (Bon Aqua, Tennessee) calls her Granny and shares that she has the most patient and caring heart—a constant caregiver to anyone who's in need. The Sullivan kids always loved to stay at their grandparents' house, and Jennifer remembers how sweet it was to be awakened by the smell of homemade waffles and syrup. Jennifer shares, "Every holiday, our family often bypasses desserts, looking for Granny's rolls. Knowing how much everyone loves them, I wanted to capture this recipe exactly how Granny does it. So before I made them the first time, I attempted to get precise instructions from Granny, though she is someone who typically doesn't measure anything—she cooks from experience and from her gut. I could hardly wait to try my attempt and see how my rolls compared to hers. My rolls on the first attempt were not nearly as good as Granny's, so I knew I must've missed something in the directions. Eager to get them right, I asked Granny if I could watch her make the rolls so I could double-check what I had written down. I immediately realized what I had done wrong! While Granny had indicated five tablespoons of shortening were needed, she neglected to mention that it was five HEAPING tablespoons—basically equivalent to half a container of Crisco. I burst out laughing as I told her how precisely I had measured my five tablespoons. HEAPING definitely made the difference! Still, no matter how often I make these rolls, nothing will ever compare with the taste of Granny making her very own."

---

5 heaping tablespoons vegetable shortening (read story above), plus extra to prepare container and baking pan

I cup whole milk

3/4 cup sugar, divided

2 (.25 ounce) packets yeast

1/4 cup lukewarm water

2 cups cold water (additional cubes of ice may be required)

3 cups all-purpose flour (or more as needed), plus extra for rolling out dough

---

1 In a saucepan over medium heat, add the shortening, milk, and 1/4 cup of the sugar and bring to a slight boil.

2 While the mixture is heating on the stove, pour the yeast packets into a medium bowl and fill with the lukewarm water and the remaining $1/2$ cup sugar, and mix. Let it sit until the shortening mixture begins to slightly boil. Make sure the sugar dissolves.

3 Remove the shortening mixture from the heat and add 2 cups of cold water to bring it to a lukewarm temperature. (You may add ice cubes to help cool it down.)

4 Combine the shortening and yeast mixtures and mix well. Add enough flour to the combined mixture to make a soft dough.

5 Place the dough into a greased, seal-tight container so the dough can rise and double in size, approximately 12 hours.

6 Once the dough has risen, preheat the oven to 350 degrees and grease a 9 x 11-inch baking pan.

7 On a floured surface, roll the dough out as you would for biscuits, and cut out rolls with a 2-inch round cutter. Take the cut dough and barely stretch it. Fold it in half and place it upright in the greased baking pan. Once the pan is full, place in the oven and bake until the rolls are golden brown on top, approximately 20 minutes.

MAKES APPROXIMATELY 30 ROLLS.

SWEET POTATO BISCUITS ✕ ✕ ✕

GEORGE KILLGORE (Nashville, Tennessee) remembers his grandmother, RADA DRAIN (Chattanooga, Tennessee), as an honest, simple, country woman who taught him that he's only as good as his word, so it had better be honorable. While she did not have a college education, she always told her grandkids to stay in school, and they all did. (Partly, George thinks, out of fear that she would jerk a knot in their tails if they didn't!) "Every summer she spent what seemed like weeks canning fresh peaches," says George. "The kitchen would be hot, and we knew to stay out of her way. Then, weeks later, when the peaches had time to 'cure,' we would reap the reward of her hard work. I could have eaten the entire jar if she would've let me. Biscuit making was her specialty. We always had hot biscuits on the table, and they were perfect every time," George adds.

Cooking spray	3/4 teaspoon salt	2/3 cup whole milk
2 cups all-purpose flour	4 tablespoons brown sugar, divided	1/2 cup mashed cooked sweet potatoes
1 tablespoon baking powder	3 tablespoons vegetable shortening	1/3 cup sour cream

1 Preheat the oven to 400 degrees. Lightly spray a cookie sheet.
2 In a medium bowl combine the flour, baking powder, salt, and 2 tablespoons of the brown sugar. With a pastry blender or 2 forks, cut the shortening into the flour mixture until it resembles coarse meal.
3 In a separate bowl combine the milk, sweet potatoes, and sour cream, blending well. Stir into the flour mixture just until moistened.
4 Drop the dough by 1/4 cupfuls onto the prepared cookie sheet. Sprinkle the tops evenly with the remaining brown sugar.
5 Bake 16 to 18 minutes or until golden brown. Remove immediately from the cookie sheet and serve warm.

MAKES 6 BISCUITS.

GRANNY PEARL'S HOMEMADE ROLLS

LYNETTE SESLER (Nashville, Tennessee) was born in Charlotte, Tennessee, also where her grandmother, VERA PEARL CORLEW, was born and raised. Vera was known as Granny Pearl to her five grandchildren. Lynette shares that "Granny Pearl always put family and God first and foremost in her life. She passed these characteristics on to my dear, sweet mother, and I am so thankful she did. Granny Pearl was a great example of strength and courage. And when it came to the kitchen, I remember these homemade rolls and the way she'd cook a grilled cheese sandwich—she'd let the cheese ooze out of the sandwich, causing it to burn on the edges. They tasted like no one else's." Granny Pearl passed away in 1976.

2 cups whole milk	2 (.25 ounce) packages yeast	extra for rolling out dough
2/3 cup vegetable shortening	3 cups self-rising flour, divided, plus	Butter to grease pan
1/2 cup sugar		

1 In a large saucepan stir together the milk, shortening, and sugar and bring nearly to a boil. Set aside and cool to lukewarm.

2 Remove 1/2 cup of the mixture, put in a small bowl, and add both packs of yeast. Stir until dissolved. Add the dissolved yeast mixture back to the reserved liquid. Add 2 cups of the flour to make a thick batter.

3 Let the batter rise approximately 2 hours or until doubled. Then add 1 cup of the flour to make the dough, and mix well. Either refrigerate for later use or make the rolls.

4 TO MAKE THE ROLLS, preheat the oven to 365 degrees. Place the dough on a lightly floured surface (preferably a biscuit board). Knead the dough until it is easy to roll out with your rolling pin. Cut out rolls with a 2-inch biscuit or round cookie cutter and place in a buttered 9 x 13-inch pan. Bake for approximately 20 minutes or until lightly browned.

MAKES ABOUT 24 ROLLS.

MAMIE'S OVERNIGHT ROLLS ✕ ✕ ✕

MINDY LEE HENDERSON (Franklin, Tennessee) describes her grandma, MAMIE LEE BOOTH (Nashville, Tennessee), as perfect, petite, and feisty! Mindy was named after Mamie and has fond memories of her dancing to music from the radio and sitting with her feet over the heat vent when she would rest. From her earliest memories, she can see Mamie in the kitchen, rolling out the dough for these rolls with a rolling pin that Mamie's dad had made for her mother. Mindy shares, "We never sat down to eat without a huge plate of rolls on the table. Mamie would make these rolls tea-size . . . so I could safely eat six each meal without thinking a thing about it. And I had my tradition—three with butter and honey and three with milk gravy. Mamie went to heaven at the age of ninety-seven, and she filled my heart with many sweet memories. Not only do I have this delicious recipe, but tucked away safe and secure is that hand-carved rolling pin that has been passed down through the generations of my family."

3/4 cup sugar

1 cup vegetable shortening, plus extra for preparing pans

2 cups water, divided

2 (.25 ounce) packages yeast

2 large eggs, slightly beaten

6 cups all-purpose flour

1 tablespoon salt

---

1 In a large bowl melt the sugar and shortening in 1 1/2 cups of the hot water; let cool.

2 Dissolve the yeast in the remaining 1/2 cup of warm water (use a yeast thermometer to make sure the water is between 110 and 115 degrees). Add the yeast and eggs to the shortening mixture. Add the flour and salt and stir with a wooden spoon. No kneading is required.

3 Let the dough rise overnight in a large bowl in the refrigerator.

4 Roll into the desired shape (round or crescent) and place on greased pans, baking trays, or muffin pans. Let rise 1 1/2 to 2 hours.

5 Preheat the oven to 350 degrees and bake 8 to 10 minutes or until lightly browned on top.

MAKES 4 DOZEN ROLLS.

VALLIE'S FROM-SCRATCH BANANA BREAD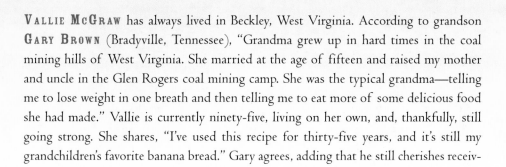

VALLIE McGRAW has always lived in Beckley, West Virginia. According to grandson GARY BROWN (Bradyville, Tennessee), "Grandma grew up in hard times in the coal mining hills of West Virginia. She married at the age of fifteen and raised my mother and uncle in the Glen Rogers coal mining camp. She was the typical grandma—telling me to lose weight in one breath and then telling me to eat more of some delicious food she had made." Vallie is currently ninety-five, living on her own, and, thankfully, still going strong. She shares, "I've used this recipe for thirty-five years, and it's still my grandchildren's favorite banana bread." Gary agrees, adding that he still cherishes receiving a loaf of this delicious bread from her.

Cooking spray

6 medium bananas, ripened

1 tablespoon butter, softened

1 tablespoon vegetable shortening

2 cups sugar

3 large eggs

4 cups all-purpose flour

2 teaspoons baking soda

1 1/2 teaspoons salt

1 cup chopped pecans

Light corn syrup

1 Preheat the oven to 350 degrees. Lightly spray two large loaf pans.
2 In a large bowl cream together the bananas, butter, shortening, and sugar. Add the eggs, flour, baking soda, salt, and pecans and stir well.
3 Pour into the loaf pans. Bake for 45 minutes or until a toothpick inserted in the center comes out clean. Brush the tops of the loaves with the corn syrup while still warm.

MAKES 2 LOAVES.

Cheesy Bubble Bread

Party Time Cheese Ball

Appetizer Meatballs

Cream Cheese-Date Nut
   Sandwiches

Nana's Ham and Cheesies
   (a.k.a. Party Sandwiches)

Spiced Pecans

Mammy's Ham Devils

Chicken-Rice Salad

Frozen Champagne Salad

Crispy Slaw

7-Up Salad

Potato Salad

Memaw's Strawberry Salad

Granny Crabtree's Pea Salad

Grey's Gulf Shores Salad

Summertime Favorite Potato Salad

Norma's Strawberry Pretzel Salad

K. K.'s Marinated Cucumbers

Other Mother's Cabbage Toss

Sausage and Bean Chowder

Grandma's Green Bean Soup

Broccoli Cheese Soup

Nama's Potato Soup

Nannaner's Brunswick Stew

Barbara's Cauliflower Cheese Soup

Grandma's Mild Chilla (a.k.a.
   Chili)

Texas Sweet Pickles

Appetizers, Soups, and Salads

CHEESY BUBBLE BREAD

KATHY WILLIAMS (Murfreesboro, Tennessee) always took her son to Sunday school while she went to "big church." Now, her son has two daughters of his own, and he takes them (Kathy's granddaughters) to Sunday school, and they love it! SYDNEE HARRIS (also of Murfreesboro) shares that her Grandma Kathy is a smart and talented woman. Sydnee and her older sister love to go to Grandma's house and swim in the pool. "My daddy also hopes my sister and I will one day grow to love Grandma's cheesy baked red potatoes and asparagus with hollandaise sauce as much as he does," Sydnee adds.

I loaf French bread

½ cup (1 stick) butter, softened or partially melted

1 (6.5 ounce) container soft spreadable cheese*

1 ½ cups shredded Italian blend cheese**

2 tablespoons fresh parsley, finely chopped

1 Preheat the oven to 400 degrees.
2 Horizontally cut the loaf of French bread in half and place both sides on a cookie sheet with the cut side up. Spread the butter and then the soft spreadable cheese evenly on each half. Sprinkle shredded cheese on each half and top with parsley. Cover the bread with foil and bake for 35 minutes.
3 Remove from the oven and change the oven setting to high broil. Remove the foil from the bread and broil for 1 minute or until the cheese has completely melted and begins to bubble. Remove from the oven and carefully slice the bread in diagonal pieces and serve. Store leftovers in the refrigerator in a sealed plastic bag or freeze.

MAKES 8 SERVINGS.

* Grandma suggests Alouette® Garlic & Herbs for the spreadable cheese.

** Use any blend of the following for the shredded cheese: mozzarella, provolone, Parmesan, Fontina, Romano, or Asiago.

PARTY TIME CHEESE BALL ✕✕✕

WILDA DOWNEY DEDRICK (Mobile, Alabama) called this her "party time" cheese ball because it was her go-to appetizer to take to parties. Wilda was known as MawMaw to her grandchildren. Sadly, she passed away in 2007 before ELI MCCOY (Hermitage, Tennessee) was born. According to Eli's mom (Gwen Dedrick McCoy) and older brother (Gray), though, MawMaw was outgoing, enjoyed making people laugh, and was always ready to be silly with the kids.

I pound shredded cheese (preferably Cheddar)

2 pounds cream cheese, softened

1 1/2 cups chopped pecans

2 large cloves garlic, minced

I teaspoon salt

1/2 cup evaporated milk

Pinch of baking soda

1/4 to 1/2 cup chopped olives (more or less depending on your preference)

1 Mix the shredded cheese, cream cheese, I cup of the pecans, garlic, salt, milk, baking soda, and olives by hand. Refrigerate for 2 to 4 hours to firm up the mixture.

2 Form into the desired shape or shapes. (It works well in one large football shape for tailgating or in two smaller round balls.) Press the remaining 1/2 cup pecans into the formed cheese ball(s) for topping and decoration. Serve with crackers.

MAKES 1 LARGE OR 2 SMALL CHEESE BALLS.

APPETIZER MEATBALLS ✕ ✕ ✕

Though **GERI WASKIEWICZ** (Spring Hill, Tennessee) has been in the South for the last twenty years, she was born in Wilkes-Barre, Pennsylvania. She has three grandchildren, all of whom live in Tennessee. Her oldest grandson, **J. J. DUBIN** (Nashville, Tennessee), loves doing things with his grandma and especially enjoys when he gets to spend the night at her house. And according to J. J.'s mom (Linda Waskiewicz Dubin), "Grandma and J. J. are always in the kitchen together, making cookies, homemade ice cream, and all sorts of treats."

I pound ground beef

I pound ground turkey

I large egg

1/2 cup bread crumbs

I teaspoon onion powder

I teaspoon garlic powder

I teaspoon dried oregano

I teaspoon crushed basil

1/2 teaspoon salt

1/2 teaspoon black pepper

I 1/2 cups tomato sauce* (for cooking in a slow cooker only)

1 In a large bowl combine the beef, turkey, egg, bread crumbs, onion powder, garlic powder, oregano, basil, salt, and pepper by hand. Form the meat mixture into 25 to 30 (1-inch) balls.

2 If baking, preheat the oven to 350 degrees. Place about 1 inch apart in a 9 x 13-inch casserole dish. Bake for 40 minutes, turning once during the baking process. When the center is no longer pink, remove from the oven and blot on paper towels to remove any grease. Add toothpicks and serve warm as an appetizer with your favorite sauce for dipping.

3 If using a slow cooker, place the formed meatballs into a slow cooker. Cover the meatballs with the tomato sauce and cook on low to medium heat for 6 to 8 hours, stirring occasionally. Serve warm as an appetizer.

MAKES 10 TO 12 APPETIZER SERVINGS.

NOTE: *Leftover meatballs are great for sandwiches or as an accompaniment to your favorite pasta and sauce.*

* Instead of tomato sauce, you can substitute a mixture of 1 bottle (12 ounce) of Heinz Chili Sauce and 12 ounces of grape jelly and follow the slow cooker cooking instructions.

✕✕ CREAM CHEESE-DATE NUT SANDWICHES

"Sometimes the smallest thing that seems insignificant can actually be a huge eye-opener, or even a whisper from God—you just have to be open to hearing it" is advice that ANN WILLHOIT (Ruther Glen, Virginia) treasures from her Grammy, ESTHER ELAINE FERKAN GREGG (Lexington, Kentucky). Ann shares that Grammy made the most beautiful and delicious angel food cake she's ever had or seen. The icing looked and tasted as light and fluffy as the cake did. Ann remembers Grammy always making one for her mother's birthday because it was her favorite too. It was also Grammy who started the family's Christmastime tradition of making and sharing pizzelles—thin, light, unique Italian cookies made with an iron press. "She passed her pizzelle press and recipe to my mom, who then passed it to my sister Leigh and me. The original machine is in Leigh's possession now, and she has truly taken the role of making them for the masses and mailing them out. I've found a more modern pizzelle press to use, but it doesn't compare to Grammy's original," Ann adds.

1 tablespoon honey	⅓ cup chopped dates	8 slices raisin bread
1 (3 ounce) package cream cheese, softened	¼ cup chopped walnuts	

1 In a medium bowl use a hand mixer to beat the honey into the cream cheese. Add the chopped dates and walnuts. Mix well with a spoon. Spread thickly onto 4 slices of raisin bread. Top with the remaining 4 slices of bread. Trim the crusts and cut each sandwich diagonally into 4 small finger sandwiches. (For a crunchier sandwich, try toasting the raisin bread.)

MAKES 4 SERVINGS.

NANA'S HAM AND CHEESIES (A.K.A. PARTY SANDWICHES)

Siblings KATHERINE PAIGE and JACKSON CAMPBELL HELTSLEY (Nashville, Tennessee) call their grandmother, DANNA LAUGHLIN (Murfreesboro, Tennessee), Nana. Nana adapted these simple, flavorful party sandwiches from a recipe used by her husband's step-mother, Ruth Laughlin, for many years. Kate and Jack love these sandwiches and have renamed them Nana's Ham and Cheesies. They are just the right size for little fingers and to serve for grown-up appetizers.

1 tray (12 each) finger-size dinner rolls in tin pan	6 slices American cheese	2 tablespoons onion flakes
12 slices thinly sliced ham	1 stick butter	2 tablespoons brown sugar
	2 tablespoons poppy seeds	2 tablespoons yellow mustard

1 Preheat the oven to 300 degrees.
2 Remove the rolls from the package and slice in half lengthwise. Fold the ham slices in half and then in half again. Place one folded square on the bottom half of each roll. Quarter the 6 slices of cheese to make 24 small squares. Place 2 squares of cheese on top of the folded ham on each roll. Place the sandwiches back into the foil tin they came in.
3 In a small saucepan combine the butter, poppy seeds, onion flakes, brown sugar, and mustard together and heat on medium until hot and thoroughly blended. Brush the heated mixture over the tops of the sandwiches.
4 Cover the tin completely with foil and bake for approximately 20 minutes or until the sandwiches are heated well through. Serve warm.

MAKES 12 SERVINGS.

 # SPICED PECANS

MELODY BARLOW (Murfreesboro, Tennessee) was born in Memphis, Tennessee. Her paternal grandmother was MYRTLE TRULL, affectionately known as Mamaw to her grandchildren. Mamaw was born and raised in Humboldt, Tennessee, and lived in Jackson, Tennessee, until she passed away in 1979. Melody shares that "based on the delicious food she made, she certainly taught me that 'from scratch' cooking is the best!"

Cooking spray

1 large egg white

1 teaspoon cold water

1 pound large pecan halves

1/2 cup sugar

1/4 teaspoon salt

1 teaspoon ground cinnamon

1 Preheat the oven to 225 degrees. Lightly spray a cookie sheet.

2 In a large bowl beat the egg white and water until frothy. Add the pecans, tossing to coat well.

3 Mix the sugar, salt, and cinnamon in another large bowl. Fold the pecans into the sugar mixture until well coated.

4 Spread in a single layer on the cookie sheet. Bake for one hour, turning every 15 minutes. Cool before serving. Store in an airtight container.

MAKES 1 POUND.

RUTHANNA MONGER was born in Columbus, Ohio, but she lived most of her life in Sweetwater, Tennessee. She was known to her eleven grandchildren as Mammy. Mammy had a rocking chair in her kitchen and a swing on her screened-in porch. Granddaughter JANET TRACY (Franklin, Tennessee) shares that "Mammy spent a lot of time rocking and swinging with her grandchildren. As kids, we had so much fun when all of the cousins would meet at Mammy's for a visit. Countless hours were spent building forts in the dining room, hiding in the cabinets, and playing dress up. Today we call the clan of cousins 'Monger Madness,' and we still get together every other year for a visit. I learned the importance of family and staying in touch from Mammy. We all appreciate her for having us get together so often and stay so close." Mammy passed away in 2006.

6 large hard-boiled eggs	1 teaspoon prepared mustard	1/2 teaspoon caraway seeds
2 tablespoons cream cheese, softened	1 teaspoon lemon juice	1/8 teaspoon salt
2 tablespoons mayonnaise	3/4 teaspoon dill	3 tablespoons cooked ham, finely chopped

1 Slice the eggs in half lengthwise and place on a serving dish. Remove the yolks and place them in a medium bowl.

2 Mash the yolks and add the cream cheese, mayonnaise, mustard, and lemon juice. Stir until smooth. Mix in the dill, caraway seeds, salt, and ham. Spoon onto the boiled egg halves. Refrigerate for at least two hours and serve cold.

MAKES 12 SERVINGS.

CHICKEN-RICE SALAD

TOBIN ORENDORF (Marietta, Georgia) shares that his Grammy, **LYNNE LOUISE NIELSEN BROWN** (Duluth, Georgia), loves to visit and always wants to know what he's learned lately. Tobin is a big storyteller, and Grammy always has a listening ear. Their time together usually involves Grammy watching him swim, reading stories, and playing with puzzles. Tobin reminds Grammy a lot of her youngest son, Dan (Tobin's uncle), when he was a little boy.

2 cups cooked chicken breast, cut into bite-size pieces

2/3 cup wild rice, cooked and cooled

2/3 cup mayonnaise

1/3 cup milk (whole or 2 percent)

1/3 cup lemon juice

2 tablespoons grated onion

8 ounces chopped artichoke hearts (optional)

1 cup chopped cashews or Grape-Nuts cereal

1 In a medium bowl add the chicken and stir in the rice.
2 In a large bowl, blend the mayonnaise, milk, lemon juice, onion, and artichoke hearts. Add the chicken and rice and mix well.
3 Refrigerate for approximately 1 hour before serving. Top with chopped cashews or Grape-Nuts right before serving.

MAKES 5 SERVINGS.

FROZEN CHAMPAGNE SALAD

CAROL FAY MASSEY was born and raised in Lafayette, Tennessee, and lived in Germany when **NATASHA STONEKING'S** (Nashville, Tennessee) grandfather was stationed there in the navy. Life then took them to Illinois, then finally back home to Tennessee to raise their three daughters. Gran and Papa (as they're known to their grandchildren) have been together for fifty-four years and currently live in Nashville. Natasha's middle name is Carol, after Gran, and Natasha's firstborn daughter is Caroline, also in honor of Gran. "Everyone who knows my Gran knows that no food is better than hers, which is why we always love gathering around her table and enjoying her incredible meals. She helped teach me how to cook at an early age, and now I am always trying to re-create her recipes that have become my favorites. At Christmastime she makes batches and batches of chocolate candy and divinity. Funny enough, no one can seem to master her divinity recipe, but I am on a mission to try this year because it's something I want to be able to carry on for my children someday too," Natasha says.

8 ounces cream cheese, softened

1 (16 ounce) can crushed pineapple, drained

1 (16 ounce) package frozen strawberries, partially thawed

1 cup pecans, chopped

3/4 cup sugar

2 large bananas, sliced in quarters

1 (8 ounce) container whipped topping

1 Mix together the cream cheese, pineapple, strawberries, pecans, and sugar. Fold in the bananas and whipped topping and pour into a 9 x 9-inch square container* with an airtight lid. Place in the freezer for at least 4 hours or freeze overnight.

2 To serve, remove the lid and let stand at room temperature for 15 to 30 minutes (just until it starts to thaw around the edges). Serve slightly frozen. Use a plastic knife to cut into individual servings. Cover remaining salad and place back into the freezer for up to 1 week.

MAKES 8 SERVINGS.

* Smaller containers will yield thicker portions.

 # CRISPY SLAW

While **KATHLEEN GANDY SHEFFIELD** was born in White Settlement, Texas, her first-born grandchild **ISABEL "IZZY" KATHLEEN SHEFFIELD** (Nashville, Tennessee) loves that her Grandma now lives close to her and her sister in Nashville. In fact, it's close enough that Grandma and PawPaw are the girls' favorite babysitters. Izzy shares that when she turned two, it was Grandma and PawPaw who bought her a pretty pink tricycle, complete with all the must-have accessories a girl could want.

I large cabbage	I teaspoon salt	½ cup salad oil*
I medium or large onion	I teaspoon celery seed	½ cup white vinegar
½ cup sugar	½ teaspoon dry mustard	

1 Shred the cabbage and onion in a food processor. Cover with the sugar.

2 Bring the salt, celery seed, mustard, salad oil, and vinegar to a boil and pour over the cabbage mixture. Mix well and store in the refrigerator. This will keep well up to 2 weeks.

MAKES 6 SERVINGS.

* Salad oil is a catch-all term for any neutral-tasting oil, such as canola, vegetable, safflower, or sunflower. Feel free to use your favorite oil in this recipe.

While she currently resides in Naperville, Illinois, ELIZABETH "LIB" BOWMAN HAUSER was born and raised in Liberty, North Carolina. She called her grandmother Grandma Mac. ALIVIE ELIZABETH BRYAN McPHERSON was born and raised on a dairy farm in Burlington, North Carolina, and later lived in Liberty until she passed away in 1943. Lib says her mom and grandma made this salad for church socials at the Pleasant Union Methodist Church in Liberty.

1 (3 ounce) box lemon gelatin

1 cup boiling water

1 (8 ounce) package cream cheese, softened

1 (8 ounce) can crushed pineapple

1 teaspoon sugar

1 teaspoon vanilla extract

1/2 cup chopped pecans

1 cup 7-Up or other lemon-lime soda

1 Pour the gelatin into a small bowl. Pour the boiling water into the bowl and dissolve the gelatin. Allow it to cool slightly, approximately 3 minutes.

2 In a medium glass bowl, cream the cream cheese and then pour in the gelatin. Beat until smooth.

3 Stir in the pineapple, sugar, vanilla, and pecans and mix well. Slowly pour in the 7-Up and stir gently.

4 Refrigerate for 3 to 4 hours before serving. Stir the mixture a couple of times during that period.

MAKES 8 SERVINGS.

POTATO SALAD ✕ ✕ ✕

SHERRIE CUNNINGHAM was born and raised in Nashville and currently resides in Old Hickory, Tennessee. Her Grandma, JOSAPHINE CATIGNANI (also of Nashville), loved to cook for her very large family—large as in seventy-eight grandchildren—especially on Sundays! Sherrie remembers that Grandma Josaphine always said that family was the most important thing and that there was nothing like a good home-cooked meal. She passed away in 1978.

---

12 medium red or white potatoes	1 tablespoon sugar	1/2 teaspoon salt
1/2 pound sliced bacon	3 tablespoons chopped onion	1/4 teaspoon black pepper
3 ounces vinegar	1 tablespoon prepared mustard	1/2 teaspoon celery salt

---

1 Place the potatoes in a large pot and fill with enough water to cover. Bring to a boil and then cook for about 10 minutes, or until easily pierced with a fork. Drain and allow to cool; then peel and slice thin.

2 Fry the bacon slices; remove from the skillet, saving the grease. Drain the cooked bacon on paper towels to blot off the grease.

3 To the hot bacon grease, add the vinegar, sugar, and onions, and sauté for approximately 90 seconds until the onions are tender.

4 Break or cut the cooked bacon into bite-size pieces. Add it to the potato slices along with the mustard, salt, black pepper, and celery salt. Stir until blended and then pour the bacon grease mixture over the potatoes. Mix well. Serve warm.

MAKES 6 TO 8 SERVINGS.

MEMAW'S STRAWBERRY SALAD

ALYSSA CUNNINGHAM (Old Hickory, Tennessee) was born in Hermitage, Tennessee, and shares that her Memaw, **SHERRIE CUNNINGHAM** (also of Old Hickory), has been there for her all her life. "If you don't believe in angels, then you haven't met my Memaw. She has been my guide through life. Everything she cooks is with love, and I especially like her special holiday dishes," Alyssa shares. Memaw has shared much with Alyssa about their family history and recipes and taught her that your best friends are your family. Memaw's strawberry salad is Alyssa's favorite dish.

1 1/4 cups water

2 (3 ounce) boxes strawberry banana gelatin

2 (10 ounce) boxes frozen strawberries, in juice

1 (16 ounce) can crushed pineapple, drained

4 medium bananas

1 (16 ounce) container sour cream

1 cup chopped pecans (optional)

1 In a saucepan boil the water. In a large bowl add the gelatin. Pour water over the gelatin and mix well. Add the strawberries, pineapple, and bananas and mix well.

2 Pour half of the mixture into an 8 x 11-inch dish, and freeze for 35 to 40 minutes or until firm.

3 Remove from the freezer and cover with sour cream. Pour the remaining mixture over the sour cream and refrigerate overnight. Top with pecans before serving.

MAKES 10 TO 12 SERVINGS.

GRANNY CRABTREE'S PEA SALAD

ANGIE CRABTREE REYNOLDS (Nashville, Tennessee) shares that her childhood was divided between her birthplace, Jackson, Mississippi, and Newport, Arkansas. Her Granny was **MARY JANE CRABTREE**, who was born in Dewitt, Arkansas, and later lived in Wynne, Arkansas, until she passed away in 1989. Angie says she was born to cook because it is in her genes. "My dad's side of the family is full of good cooks—from my uncle who owned a well-known barbecue restaurant, to an aunt who was a cookbook author and catered for the set of the movie *The Four Seasons*, to my dad, whose peanut butter fudge won a recipe contest. But it was their mom and my Granny who inspired us all." Regrettably, Angie didn't discover her love of cooking until after her Granny passed away, so she never took advantage of working side by side with her in the kitchen. But luckily, she has many memories of the foods that Granny cooked for her family over the years and loves knowing they have a shared joy of cooking. Angie remembers this pea salad being at every meal her Granny made, and Angie's dad absolutely loves it!

2 (8.5 ounce) cans English peas, drained

1 (4 ounce) jar pimentos, drained

1 (8 ounce) can pineapple chunks, drained

3 large hard-boiled eggs, chopped

3/4 cup Miracle Whip salad dressing (or more to taste)

1 Mix the peas, pimentos, pineapple chunks, eggs, and Miracle Whip together, and chill for approximately 2 hours before serving.

MAKES 6 SERVINGS.

GREY'S GULF SHORES SALAD

Her grandparents bought a driftwood-tinted beach house on the sugar-white beaches of Gulf Shores, Alabama, in 1978, shares HANNAH TURNER LAVEY (Nashville, Tennessee). Her ninety-four-year-old grandmother, GWYNDOLYN COLLINS TURNER, affectionately known as Grey, still travels down to the coast each season to feel the gulf breezes, listen to the seagulls, and make her favorite seafood dish: this salad. Her husband, David (whom the grandchildren called GrandDavid), did not like most of the catch from the Gulf, but he adored this dish, as did her six grandchildren. Grey would serve it in bowls, with saltine crackers on the side. "My grandmother is not only an amazing cook but one of the most beautiful, intelligent, and sophisticated ladies I know. At the beach, she would read books to us aloud with her Southern lilt, batting her deep-hooded eyes with dramatic effect. Whether at the beach house, at her home in Demopolis, or over the phone, Grey never ceases to make her grandchildren and six great-grandchildren feel as if they are simply the most marvelous people in the world," Hannah says.

---

1 medium onion, finely chopped	Salt and black pepper to taste	3 ounces cider vinegar
1 pound fresh lump crabmeat	4 ounces vegetable oil	4 ounces ice water

---

1 Spread half of the onion over the bottom of a large bowl. Cover with separated crab lumps and then the remaining onion. Add the salt and pepper to taste.

2 Pour the oil, vinegar, and ice water over all. Cover and marinate for 2 to 12 hours. Toss lightly before serving. Serve cold.

MAKES 4 TO 5 SERVINGS.

SUMMERTIME FAVORITE POTATO SALAD

Grandmother **JUANITA JOHNSON** (Murfreesboro, Tennessee) was known as a wonderful cook who hosted many family dinners, shares granddaughter **KRISTEN SIEBER** (also of Murfreesboro). Juanita was a grandmother to seven and enjoyed sharing her recipes. This potato salad was and still is a family favorite, especially in the summertime. Juanita was also an avid fan of cookbooks, amassing quite a collection from the United States and around the world. She passed away in 2007 and is dearly missed by all who knew her.

---

3 to 4 large potatoes

1/4 cup chopped onion

1 1/2 teaspoon salt

1/8 teaspoon black pepper

1/8 teaspoon celery seed

2 tablespoons vegetable oil

2 tablespoons vinegar

2 tablespoons chopped sweet gherkin pickles

2 tablespoons chopped green bell pepper

1/2 cup mayonnaise

1 tablespoon mustard

2 large hard-boiled eggs

---

1 Scrub the potatoes and place in a large pot of cold water. Cover and bring to a boil over high heat. Allow to cook for 30 to 40 minutes.

2 Peel the skins back and dice the warm potatoes. Sprinkle the onion over the potatoes. Add salt, pepper, and celery seed.

3 In a small bowl mix the oil and vinegar and pour over the potatoes. Cover and let sit on the counter for two hours. Add the pickles and green pepper.

4 In a small bowl mix together the mayonnaise and mustard. Stir into the potato mixture. Chop the eggs on top and mix well.

5 Refrigerate for at least two hours before serving. Serve cold and refrigerate any leftovers.

MAKES 4 TO 5 SERVINGS.

❮✕✕✕ NORMA'S STRAWBERRY PRETZEL SALAD

SCOTT CURTIS SIMS'S (Auburn, Alabama) Nana, NORMA SIMS (Nashville, Tennessee), was born and raised in Millers Creek, North Carolina. While she passed away in 2001, she's remembered for her contagious smile. Nana accepted what she had and never worried about keeping up with the Joneses—she was a great example and a giving person, helping people anytime they needed it. Scott says he admires her for taking swimming lessons for the first time in her life in her fifties. She even went on to take and pass the Red Cross Lifesaving Course, not to be a lifeguard but for survival. Nana had a gift for cooking and baking and was very happy when she prepared meals for her family and friends. Scott's been told that Nana always had food in the fridge for any unexpected visitors. When his dad and uncle were in college and came home on the weekend with a friend, Nana would have some type of cake or pie that their dad would refer to as the "two-week-old" cake. Their friends thought that was funny, and no one never turned away Nana's desserts. This salad, now made by Scott's mom when he's home from college, reminds him of Nana anytime he eats it.

FIRST LAYER:

2 cups crushed pretzels (use food processor)

3/4 cup (1 1/2 sticks) butter, melted

3 tablespoons sugar

SECOND LAYER:

1 (8 ounce) package cream cheese, softened

1 cup sugar

1 (8 ounce) container frozen whipped topping, thawed

THIRD LAYER:

1 (6 ounce) package strawberry gelatin

1 1/2 cups boiling water

2 (10 ounce) packages frozen sliced strawberries

1 Preheat the oven to 400 degrees.
2 TO MAKE THE FIRST LAYER, in a small bowl mix the pretzel crumbs, butter, and sugar. Press into a 9 x 13-inch pan.
3 Bake for 8 minutes. Cool thoroughly.

4 **To make the second layer**, in a large bowl mix the cream cheese and sugar. Fold in the whipped topping. Spread over the pretzel layer.

5 **To make the third layer**, in a medium bowl dissolve the strawberry gelatin in boiling water. Add the frozen strawberries and place in the refrigerator to chill approximately 20 minutes, until syrupy.

6 Pour the strawberries over the cream cheese layer and refrigerate approximately 2 hours, until well chilled. This can be made a day ahead. Serve cold.

MAKES 10 SERVINGS.

K. K.'S MARINATED CUCUMBERS

KATHERINE CORTNER KEELING (Nashville, Tennessee) was born, raised, and lived most of her life in and around Tullahoma, Tennessee. She is known as K. K. to her three grandchildren and Great K. K. to her six great-grandchildren. Oldest granddaughter MANDY BUTTERS (Brentwood, Tennessee) shares, "At ninety-five and still independent, my grandmother is an inspiration to everyone around. Her sunny outlook on life and colorful personality brighten every room she enters." Mandy has a lifetime of wonderful memories with her beloved K. K., from visits and trips to holidays and more delicious meals than she could ever count! "Now that I have kids, I love to take them to visit their Great K. K. on the weekends. The first thing they do is belly up to the counter for banana pudding. This is one of my favorite salads, and as the directions say, it will keep several days in the refrigerator—it gets better with age, just like K. K.," Mandy adds.

---

5 medium cucumbers	1/2 cup white vinegar	1/3 cup sugar
1 Vidalia onion, sliced	1/2 cup water	Salt and black pepper to taste

---

1 Peel and slice the cucumbers to 1/4-inch slices and place in a shallow serving dish. Add the onion slices.
2 In a jar with a tight-fitting lid, combine the vinegar, water, sugar, salt, and pepper. Shake well to combine, and pour over the cucumbers and onions.
3 Cover and marinate at least an hour; longer is better. This will keep several days in the refrigerator.

MAKES 6 TO 8 SERVINGS.

"My grandmother—I called her Other Mother—was a natural cook, knowing just how to make anything taste great," recalls **DARLENE RANDOLPH** (Nashville, Tennessee). "I remember my very first dinner party in my new apartment when I was just twenty-two years old. I had invited my mother, father, grandmother—**ROBERTA HARDCASTLE WAHL** (Goodlettsville, Tennessee)—and step-grandfather over for dinner. I had worked all day to prepare a shrimp casserole for the first time . . . and thus made a future note-to-self: always try new recipes before the main event. Anyway, being somewhat anxious, I tasted the casserole right before I was about to call them to the table, and it was awful. Panic-stricken, I asked my mother to come in and taste it. She agreed—it was awful! She in turn asked her mother (my grandmother) to come taste it. My grandmother came in, tasted the dish, and immediately got to work scanning my cupboards and refrigerator for ingredients and mixing them into the casserole. And . . . voilà! Of course, when she was finished, it was delicious. She knew all the tricks of toning down flavors, enhancing a dish, and in my case, fixing a recipe. After that dinner party, when we went to Grandmother's home for dinner, the question always was asked—'What's in it?' It became one of our family jokes and a memorable tradition."

1 large cabbage	1 cup sugar	1 tablespoon celery seed
2 medium green bell peppers, finely chopped	1 tablespoon salt	
	1 cup cider vinegar	1 tablespoon dry mustard
1 large onion, finely chopped	3/4 cup canola oil (or other mild tasting oil)	

1 Chop the cabbage very fine (in a food processor or chopper) and place in a deep bowl.
2 Place the peppers on top of the cabbage. Place the onion on top of the peppers. Do not toss.
3 Sprinkle the sugar and salt over the vegetables.
4 In a small saucepan add the vinegar, oil, celery seed, and mustard. Bring to a boil, stirring occasionally. Pour the dressing over the vegetables. Refrigerate for at least 6 hours. Toss just before serving.

MAKES 10 TO 12 SERVINGS.

NOTE: *This salad can be made as far ahead as necessary. If you aren't serving a large group, you may want to halve the recipe.*

SAUSAGE AND BEAN CHOWDER

"My Mimi, HELON BARRON STANDIFER (Dothan, Alabama), taught my dad (her son), GREG STANDIFER, to make holidays an event. And he's passed that tradition on to us," shares grandson JOSH STANDIFER (Cleveland, Tennessee). Mimi was known to impart many wise thoughts, such as, "Embrace your family and make sure they are loved, because when they are gone, there is no going back." Sadly, she passed away in 2000. But her words of wisdom live on, including: "Trust your heart and don't be afraid of life. Never forget where you came from and your family, and be yourself."

---

2 pounds pork sausage

4 cups water

1 (16 ounce) can kidney beans, undrained

2 medium onions, chopped

2 medium potatoes, peeled and cubed

$1/2$ cup chopped green bell pepper

1 large bay leaf

$1/2$ teaspoon salt

$1/2$ teaspoon whole dried thyme

$1/4$ teaspoon black pepper

---

1 Brown the sausage in a Dutch oven over medium-high heat, stirring to crumble. Cook until no pink remains. Drain off any grease.

2 Add the water, beans, onions, potatoes, green peppers, bay leaf, salt, thyme, and black pepper. Stir; then bring to a boil over medium-high heat.

3 Reduce the heat, cover, and simmer for 1 hour. Remove the bay leaf and serve hot.

MAKES 6 SERVINGS.

GRANDMA'S GREEN BEAN SOUP

"More thoup" were the words often uttered by granddaughter SOPHIA PORTER as a little girl, indicating she was ready for more soup—usually of the homemade chicken and noodles variety. And such sweet words they were for Grandma, CHARLOTTE FERKAN PORTER. Charlotte is known for making many varieties of soup—this green bean soup recipe is one of her family's favorites. And her family just happens to include daughter Faye Porter (Nashville, Tennessee), the author of this book. Charlotte has four granddaughters: Lillian, Ava, Olivia, and Sophia Porter.

2 (14.5 ounce) cans green beans, undrained, or 3 1/2 cups fresh or frozen green beans

1 tablespoon vegetable shortening or oil

2 tablespoons all-purpose flour

1 clove garlic, minced

2 slices bacon, cooked and chopped (not too crisp)

1/8 teaspoon caraway seed

1 Pour the beans and juice (if using canned beans) in a large pan or Dutch oven and allow to simmer over medium heat. Add enough water to fully cover the beans.

2 In a heavy skillet over medium to low heat, melt the shortening to make the soup base or roux. Gradually add the flour, stirring constantly. After about 2 minutes, when the base color starts to turn a light brown, add the minced garlic. Continue to stir until the base turns light to medium brown in color. Stir continuously, as the mixture can quickly burn. Remove the skillet from the heat.

3 Slowly ladle one cup of the hot bean juice from the simmering beans to the skillet. Be careful; the soup base will steam. Continue stirring carefully until the mixture is smooth.

4 Add the base mixture to the pot of simmering beans, along with the pieces of bacon and the caraway seed. Add water as necessary so the beans are always submerged under the broth.

5 Simmer on low heat for 30 minutes, stirring occasionally. Serve hot. Have a cruet of cider vinegar on the table, as a few drops in your bean soup enhance the flavor. Pass the basket of rye bread and enjoy!

MAKES 4 TO 6 SERVINGS.

BROCCOLI CHEESE SOUP XXX

"Never say a bad word about anyone" was the rule that GENEVIE FLORIDA (Lascassas, Tennessee) lived by. Granddaughter MORGAN LAMB (Murfreesboro, Tennessee) shares that her Mama Gen was known for always making cookies for the neighborhood kids. And while raising her children, she cooked every meal at home, complete with homemade bread, except for Friday nights—that was her night to eat out. Mama Gen passed on the tradition of cooking big Sunday dinners and taught her family how to make home such a special place. Morgan also shared one of Mama Gen's sayings: "The camera doesn't lie."

---

1 cup water

1 chicken bouillon cube

1 (10 ounce) package frozen broccoli

1 large carrot, grated

2 tablespoons butter

3 tablespoons all-purpose flour

2 cups whole milk

16 ounces pasteurized processed cheese, cubed

1 (14.25 ounce) can cream of chicken soup

1 tablespoon minced onion flakes

1 tablespoon Worcestershire sauce

Salt and black pepper to taste

---

1 In a medium saucepan heat the water and bouillon cube to a boil. Add the broccoli and carrot. Remove from the heat.

2 In a large saucepan make a white sauce by melting the butter and slowly stirring in the flour. Gradually add the milk and stir until thickened a bit. Add the cubed cheese, soup, onion flakes, Worcestershire sauce, and salt and pepper. Add the broccoli and carrot mixture to the white sauce mixture and cook over medium heat until thickened. Serve hot.

MAKES 4 SERVINGS.

NAMA'S POTATO SOUP ✕ ✕ ✕

CHARLOTTE LOUISE FERKAN PORTER was born in New Bethlehem, Pennsylvania. She's a mother of four and a grandmother of four. And her daughter, Faye, happens to be the author of this book. So while Charlotte doesn't live in the South, she's got two kids who live in Nashville, Tennessee. She is a grandma and a good cook who's taught Faye much of what she knows about cooking and baking. One of Charlotte's favorite Southern places to visit—next to her kids in Nashville, of course—has been the Greenbrier Resort, a national historic landmark in White Sulfur Springs, West Virginia. She loved it there so much she even bought some of their custom-made china. Charlotte is known as Nama to younger granddaughters AVA and LILLIAN PORTER and as Grandma to older granddaughters SOPHIA and OLIVIA PORTER.

---

4 large potatoes

1 teaspoon butter

1 tablespoon finely chopped onion

1/3 cup finely chopped celery leaves, packed

1/3 cup finely chopped carrot (optional)

Salt and black pepper to taste

3/4 cup cooked small macaroni, shells, or ditalini (optional)

---

1 Peel and cube the potatoes. Rinse and place in a Dutch oven or kettle. Add enough cold water to cover potatoes by less than an inch. Bring to a boil over high heat and then lower the temperature and cook over medium heat. With a large spoon remove the starchy bubbles that form on the side of the kettle.

2 While the potatoes are cooking, in a small skillet melt the butter and sauté the onions until tender. Be careful not to brown the butter. Add the sautéed onions to the potatoes, along with the celery leaves, carrot, and salt and pepper to your taste.

3 Check the potatoes after 5 minutes to make sure they are not too soft or mushy.

4 If adding cooked pasta, gently stir it in and make sure the entire mixture is covered with the broth. If too thick, add additional water until the desired consistency is achieved.

5 Lower the heat to the lowest setting and allow the flavors to incorporate for 6 to 8 minutes. Serve hot. Crusty bread goes well with this soup.

MAKES 6 SERVINGS.

✖ ✖ ✖ NANNANER'S BRUNSWICK STEW

Jamie Roberts (Nashville, Tennessee) was born in Montevallo, Alabama. She shares that her paternal grandmother, Bertie Mae Williams Roberts, was born in the small Georgia town of Millen in 1914. The grandchildren affectionately called her Nannaner. One of her specialties was Brunswick stew, a classic Georgian recipe perfectly scaled for large crowds hungry for a hearty blend of chicken, tomatoes, potatoes, corn, and onions. The dish dictates a long, slow process, so cooking it became the central event of many Roberts family social gatherings. "The family would sit around the fire, laughing at old jokes and swapping stories as the concoction thickened. We could hardly wait to ladle the piping hot stew over rice, and nobody missed a chance to use a couple of slices of barbecue bread to sop up the juice. While I've never had the patience to try making the stew myself, I'll gladly travel hundreds of miles whenever I hear my daddy has a pot simmering," Jamie says.

2 medium hens

1 pound calf liver

6 large onions, diced

2 1/2 pounds potatoes, peeled and diced

1 gallon canned tomatoes

1 gallon canned whole corn

1/2 gallon chicken broth

1 quart whole milk

1 pound butter

1 (12 ounce) bottle chili sauce

4 tablespoons Worcestershire sauce

Hot sauce to taste

Salt and black pepper to taste

1 Boil the hens for several hours.

2 In a separate pot, presoak the liver for 20 to 30 minutes, rinse, and then boil for 40 minutes. When done, drain and grind the liver into a large pot.

3 When the hens are done, remove from the boiling water, pull the meat from the bones, and shred into small pieces (as for hash). Place in the pot with the ground liver.

4 Strain the hen broth and add to the large pot with the liver and hen meat. Add the onions, potatoes, tomatoes, corn, chicken broth, milk, and butter. Cook slowly over an open flame or gas.

5 Once the stew begins to simmer, cook for 6 hours or until well thickened, stirring consistently. Add the chili and Worcestershire sauces and mix well. When ready to eat, season to your liking with hot sauce, salt, and pepper. Serve hot.

MAKES 12 TO 15 SERVINGS.

BARBARA'S CAULIFLOWER CHEESE SOUP

Laura Troup (Nashville, Tennessee) shares that her mom was one of Grandma **Barbara Coats's** (Florence, Alabama) five daughters. Grandma made sure her girls got out the door to school with a hot breakfast every morning, many of which included her homemade waffles from an old, well-worn iron. As the girls moved away one by one, breakfast got simpler and simpler. By the time the youngest daughter was in high school, Grandma was waking her up with a breakfast of Little Debbie snack cakes and Dr Pepper in bed! Laura also adds that "my grandparents owned a beautiful home that is now known as Coby Hall and is part of the campus of the University of North Alabama. Across the street from that home was a kitchen supply store. The store offered cooking classes that Grandma took advantage of. She bought a food processor and learned how to use it and started slicing vegetables. She became familiar with a delicious cauliflower soup recipe, mastered it, and made it for years."

---

4 cups hot water

3 chicken bouillon cubes

1/2 large head of cauliflower,

separated into small florets

I medium white onion, sliced

Salt to taste

1/2 cup nonfat powdered milk

I cup shredded Cheddar cheese

---

1 Add the water and bouillon cubes to a large pot. Over medium heat, dissolve the bouillon cubes. When dissolved, add the cauliflower, onion, and salt. Cover and simmer for 15 minutes. Stir in the powdered milk. Slowly add the cheese and stir until the cheese melts and the soup is heated through. Serve hot.

MAKES 3 TO 4 SERVINGS.

GRANDMA'S MILD CHILLA (A.K.A. CHILI)

Author **FAYE PORTER** (Nashville, Tennessee) shares, "My paternal grandma was **MARY GLADYS THOMAS PORTER**, born and raised in Pennsylvania. While I was just eight when she passed away, I do have a few remembrances that I mentioned in the book's introduction. I am fortunate that some of my older cousins—Carol, Karen, Susan, and Ruth Ann—have more vivid memories, recalling Grandma's old coal oven and stove that she used to seemingly produce fabulous meals out of thin air. Of particular note were Grandma Porter's noodles from scratch, tall angel food cakes, emerald green bread-and butter pickles, orange rolls, tomato sauce, and her homemade bread—reminding one cousin of a gigantic cupcake it was so high. A favorite treat could always be found in her pantry—graham crackers sandwiched around a filling of homemade powdered sugar icing mixed with peanut butter until fluffy. Grandma never had a refrigerator when she lived on the farm, so she kept food cold or made Jell-O by placing them in the springhouse drain. The water was so cold exiting the deep-dug well, and when it got full it spilled out into a drain. Grandma would place a brick or stone in the drain and set prepared Jell-O on the brick for the cold water to set it. Whoever was visiting would make the trip to the springhouse with Grandma to retrieve cold items that would be served for dinner and then would go back after the meal to leave the leftovers for safekeeping. My parents recently came across an old cookbook that was Grandma Porter's—it was published by the Rumford Baking Powder Company (copyright 1908, 1918). Inside, Grandma handwrote some of her favorite recipes on the blank pages. This 'chilla' was found in that book in her handwriting."

---

2 pounds ground beef

2 cups chopped onion

2 cloves garlic, minced

2 (15 ounce) cans tomato sauce

2 (29 ounce) cans diced tomatoes, undrained

3/4 cup water

1 teaspoon sugar

2 (16 ounce) cans red kidney beans, drained and rinsed

Salt and black pepper to taste

---

1 Heat a Dutch oven over medium-high heat. Add the ground beef and onion and sauté until the beef is browned and the onion is tender. Drain off any excess fat. Add the garlic, tomato sauce, tomatoes, water, and sugar. Bring to a boil and reduce heat to low.

2 Cover and simmer for 1 hour, stirring occasionally. Stir in the beans and simmer for an additional 30 minutes or until the beans are heated through. Add salt and pepper to taste and serve hot.

MAKES 10 TO 12 SERVINGS.

NOTE: *If you prefer a spicy chili, before boiling the mixture add 1 1/2 teaspoons ground cumin, 1/4 cup chili powder, 1 teaspoon cayenne pepper, and chopped jalapeños to your taste.*

TEXAS SWEET PICKLES

While **KENNAH MASON** now lives in Franklin, Tennessee, she comes from a strong line of Texan ladies who smile when they say, "Strong Southern women are baked best in the Texas sun." Kennah was born and raised in Dallas, Texas, and considers herself fortunate to have adult relationships with both her grandmother—**LINDA TURMAN** (Lewisville, Texas), a.k.a. Grammy—and her great-grandmother—**BILLIE BUSHONG** (also from Lewisville), a.k.a. Honey. Kennah shares, "My Honey and Grammy taught me how to be a strong woman and to rely on my faith in the Lord. I always loved these pickles because Grammy and Honey would bring them to us in Mason jars. Since that's our last name, it always felt kind of special."

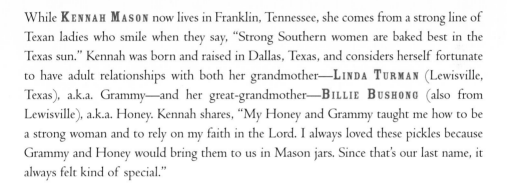

| 1 (32 ounce) jar whole dill pickles | 2 cups sugar | 1 cup cider vinegar |

1 Drain the pickles and cut into spears. Return to jar.
2 Mix the sugar and vinegar in a saucepan and bring to a boil over medium-high heat. Pour over the pickles to cover. Tightly reattach the lid and place in the refrigerator for 2 weeks. Do not reuse the vinegar from the pickles.

MAKES 1 QUART.

Christmas Sweet Potato Pudding

Vegetable Mix-up

DeeDee's Pea Casserole

Mom Mom's Brown Rice Casserole

Granny's Squash Casserole

Southern-Style Fresh Green Beans

Baked Beans à la Mimi

Grandma Fry's Noodles

Infamous Giblet Gravy

Grammy's Cheese Grits

Sara's Sweet Potato Casserole

Grammy's Hash Brown Casserole

Fried Okra and Potatoes

Grandmommy's Corn Pudding

Kentucky "Spoon Bread"

Grana's Grown-Up Mac and Cheese

MawMaw's Mac and Cheese

Mississippi Fried Corn

Nanny's Potato Pancakes

Ida's Pimento Squash Casserole

B. G.'s BBC's (a.k.a. Buttered Balsamic Carrots)

K. K.'s Rummy Sweet Potato Apple Bake

Mama Dee's Christmas Dressing

Side Dishes

❌❌❌ CHRISTMAS SWEET POTATO PUDDING

WANDA WATTS was born and raised in Detroit, Michigan, but now lives in Springfield, Tennessee. Her Mammy, LUCY ADAMS REYNOLDS (also from Springfield), passed away in 1973. She was born in Celina, Tennessee (Clay County), and married Tom Reynolds on January 17, 1920. Mammy had a green thumb, growing the most beautiful flowers—she was always taking bouquets to family, friends, and anyone who needed cheering up. Ladies came to Mammy's home from all over the county to get flower cuttings from her and to get advice on how to grow certain types of flowers.

Vegetable shortening to prepare dish

1 cup whole milk

3 cups cooked sweet potatoes cut into small pieces

1 1/2 cups sugar

1/2 cup (1 stick) butter, melted

1 teaspoon nutmeg

2 teaspoons ground cinnamon

1/2 teaspoon allspice

---

1 Preheat the oven to 350 degrees. Grease a 2-quart baking dish.
2 Pour the milk into a large bowl. Grate the potatoes into the milk. Add the sugar, butter, nutmeg, cinnamon, and allspice and blend with a hand mixer. Transfer to the dish and bake uncovered for 55 to 60 minutes or until firm.

MAKES 6 SERVINGS.

VEGETABLE MIX-UP ✕ ✕ ✕

ELIZABETH "BETSY" WATTS KOCH (Brentwood, Tennessee) was born in Chicago, Illinois, and raised in Nashville, Tennessee. Her Granny, LAURA FRANCES HARRIS WATTS (also from Nashville), was raised to be a Southern belle, but she didn't start cooking until she was about fifty, after her mother died. Betsy remembers liking some of Granny's kitchen tools, which she thinks belonged to Laura's mother. She especially liked her nonelectric beaters, which had a flywheel you turned, which then turned the beaters. Betsy shares, "The weekend before Granny had a major stroke in 1980, she and the rest of my family visited me in New Orleans for parents' weekend at Tulane. We were all in the French Quarter, and I remember both of my grandmothers standing in the middle of Bourbon Street with their mouths hanging open as they stared at some of the interesting characters that passed by. I do remember once after a stroke when one of her rare sentences burst out: 'I'm full as a Billy goat.'" Granny passed away in 1990.

---

1 (10 ounce) package frozen green beans, cooked per package directions

1 (10 ounce) package peas, cooked per package directions

1 (10 ounce) package lima beans, cooked per package directions

1 1/2 cups mayonnaise

1 small onion, grated

3 large hard-boiled eggs, chopped

3 tablespoons vegetable oil

Dash of salt

Dash of hot sauce

Paprika (optional)

---

1 Drain the green beans, peas, and lima beans, and mix together with the mayonnaise, onions, eggs, oil, salt, and hot sauce. You can either refrigerate and serve cold or cover and bake at 350 degrees for 30 minutes. In true '60s spirit, sprinkle with paprika before serving.

MAKES 10 TO 12 SERVINGS.

✕✕✕ DEEDEE'S PEA CASSEROLE

DORIS DAVIS NORMENT (Whiteville, Tennessee) was known as DeeDee to her grand-children. Granddaughter LAURA CREEKMORE (Nashville, Tennessee) remembers, "Every year at Thanksgiving, we all gathered at my parents' house growing up. Inevitably, after dinner, the men would leave the table to go watch football, and the women would stay around the table to drink more iced tea and visit. DeeDee would usually sit quietly and listen to all the stories and tales that were told. One year, after several particularly raucous stories about various family members and acquaintances, DeeDee said, 'I tell you what. I sure am glad I'm here.' We all expected her to add something to the effect of how nice it was to visit with family. Instead, she finished, 'Because you all would surely be talking about me like this if I weren't.' It still makes me laugh today to think about that. She had that kind of cutting wit—she could see right through your pretense and still laugh along with you," Laura adds. This casserole recipe is a Thanksgiving favorite in Laura's family.

CASSEROLE:

Vegetable shortening to prepare dish

1/2 cup (1 stick) butter

1 small onion, minced

2 tablespoons diced green bell pepper

1 cup sliced celery

2 (8.5 ounce) cans* English peas, drained

1 (8 ounce) can sliced water chestnuts, undrained

1 (14.25 ounce) can cream of mushroom soup

1 (4 ounce) jar diced pimentos, drained

TOPPING:

2 tablespoons butter, melted

1 cup bread crumbs

1 Preheat the oven to 350 degrees. Grease a 2-quart casserole dish.
2 TO MAKE THE CASSEROLE, melt the butter in a medium skillet over medium heat. Sauté the onion, green pepper, and celery until tender.
3 In a large bowl add the peas, water chestnuts, cream of mushroom soup, and pimentos. Transfer the mixture to the casserole dish and bake for 50 minutes. Remove from the oven.

3 To make the topping, in a small bowl toss the butter with the bread crumbs. Sprinkle on top of the casserole and bake for an additional 10 minutes. Serve warm.

MAKES 6 TO 8 SERVINGS.

* Or the equivalent amount of frozen peas

MOM MOM'S BROWN RICE CASSEROLE ✕✕✕

JARED HENDERSON (Franklin, Tennessee) shares that his very favorite thing to eat when he was growing up was his Mom Mom's Brown Rice Casserole. Prior to each birthday she'd call to confirm what he wanted her to make for his birthday dinner, and she would say, "I know you want the brown rice casserole." The whole family gets together once a month, and every time, without fail, the casserole is there. On arrival, Jared can count on a hug from Mom Mom as she whispers, "Your casserole is right over there." Mom Mom is CAROLYN BOOTH (Nashville, Tennessee). Carolyn has eight grandchildren and makes each one of them feel special by cooking their favorite foods.

Cooking spray	1 small (4.5 ounce) jar chopped mushrooms, drained (optional)	1/2 cup (1 stick) butter
1 cup rice, uncooked		1 small onion, chopped
2 (10.5 ounce) cans beef consommé		

1 Preheat the oven to 350 degrees.
2 Lightly grease a 2-quart casserole dish with cooking spray and add the rice, consommé, and mushrooms.
3 Melt the butter in a medium skillet over medium-high heat, and sauté the onions until translucent in color. Pour the melted butter and sautéed onions over the rice mixture. Stir until well blended.
4 Cover and bake approximately 45 minutes or until the rice is fully cooked and tender.

MAKES 6 TO 8 SERVINGS.

❌✕❌ GRANNY'S SQUASH CASSEROLE

MILES NEELY (Nashville, Tennessee) calls his grandma Granny. Granny is MARY MITCHELL (McMinnville, Tennessee). Miles loves to spend time with his Granny and Papa at their farm in McMinnville. Their favorite things to do together include camping; feeding the cows, fish, and goats; and watering the grass. And he especially likes the bucket of toys and go-cart that Granny and Papa have spoiled him with.

Vegetable shortening to prepare dish

6 medium yellow summer squash

I medium onion

1/4 cup (1/2 stick) butter, softened

4 slices American cheese

I (14.25 ounce) can cream of mushroom soup

Salt and black pepper to taste

1/2 sleeve saltine crackers (approximately 20 crackers)

1/2 cup shredded cheese (any type you prefer)

1 Preheat the oven to 400 degrees. Grease a 2-quart casserole dish.

2 Wash and slice the squash and dice the onion and add to a medium pot full of water. Bring to a boil and cook until soft, 10 to 12 minutes.

3 Drain well and return the vegetables to the pot. Add the butter and stir until melted. Tear the cheese slices and add the pieces to the pot. Add the cream of mushroom soup, and salt and pepper to your taste. Crush and add the saltine crackers. Blend all together and pour into the prepared casserole dish. Top with shredded cheese.

4 Bake for approximately 30 minutes; the casserole should be golden brown and bubbly. Serve hot.

MAKES 6 TO 8 SERVINGS.

SOUTHERN-STYLE FRESH GREEN BEANS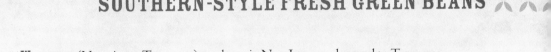

Paige Worrell (Hermitage, Tennessee) was born in New Jersey and moved to Tennessee when she was six. Her mother was born and raised in Tennessee but moved away for a few years after marrying Paige's father, a "Jersey boy." Shortly after moving back to Tennessee, Paige's mother and Grannie **Juanita Messenger** (Sparta, Tennessee) had to do a lot of coaxing to get a six-year-old to try green beans that looked different from what she had been eating. But Paige finally tried the green beans and began to look forward to them when they'd have meals with Grannie. And she adds, "I'm very thankful that I can now re-create them as an adult."

4 cups (1 quart) green beans (fresh, frozen, or canned)	1 slice of seasoning meat (bacon, ham) or a ham bone	2 (14.5 ounce) cans chicken broth Water as needed

1 Place the green beans in a pot with the seasoning meat. Pour in the chicken broth and add water to cover the beans with liquid. Simmer on medium for 1 hour. Add water as needed to keep beans covered in liquid.

2 For the next hour, let the liquid cook down in the pot to approximately half an inch; be careful not to let the pot scald or the beans stick. Check the consistency of the beans and determine remaining cooking time by the amount of water remaining in the pan. Paige usually cooks them for 1 to 2 more hours while adding water as needed. Serve warm.

MAKES 6 TO 8 SERVINGS.

Note *from Granddaughter: This recipe can be adjusted according to the amount of fresh green beans that are available. Also, Grannie adds her chicken broth at the end, while I add mine in the beginning. If you use low sodium chicken broth, I recommend using 1 can of regular chicken broth for better flavor.*

BAKED BEANS À LA MIMI XXX

"Put God first, and everything else will fall into its place" is some great advice that **HELON BARRON STANDIFER** (Dothan, Alabama) shared with her Dothan–born granddaughter, **LAUREL STANDIFER** (Franklin, Tennessee). Laurel and her brother, Josh, affectionately referred to Helon as Mimi. From Mimi, Laurel says, "I have learned that it's okay to be a strong and independent person yet still be loving, warm, and open to others. Mimi always had time for everyone and genuinely cared about those she knew and loved. I miss her." She passed away in 2000.

2 cups dry navy beans	1 teaspoon salt	1/4 cup molasses
1 1/2 quarts water	1/4 pound salt pork*	1/2 teaspoon prepared mustard

1 Wash and sort the beans by removing any bad ones or hard pieces in the bag. Rinse well and drain. Put the beans in a large Dutch oven or pot. Add the water, bring to a boil, and boil 2 minutes. Remove from the heat, cover, and let soak 1 hour.

2 Add salt, cover, and boil gently for 45 minutes.

3 Cut the salt pork into pieces about 1/2 inch thick. Add the salt pork to the beans, and cook 30 minutes longer or until the beans are tender.

4 In a small bowl mix the molasses and mustard and stir into the beans.

5 Preheat the oven to 350 degrees. Pour the beans into a 2-quart casserole dish or glazed bean pot. Bake for 1 hour or until the beans are tender and lightly browned on the top.

MAKES 6 SERVINGS.

* A large slab of bacon can be substituted if you cannot find salt pork.

✕✕✕ GRANDMA FRY'S NOODLES

TAMMY GIBSON (Springfield, Tennessee) remembers that noodles were always in demand at a Fry family gathering, with the noodle pot seemingly larger and larger with each passing Christmas. "I think my Grandma Fry, **APPIE CLEO HICKERSON FRY** (DeWitt, Missouri), spent days making and drying those noodles. When my Aunt Jenny got married, Grandma cooked a meal for the family. Grandpa told her she didn't have enough noodles, so she made more. However, it turned out to be much more than they needed. So, to get back at my grandpa for having her make so much more, on his next day back to work Grandma surprised him with a leftover noodle sandwich in his lunch! Can you imagine his reaction when he bit into that sandwich? At subsequent family gatherings, if the noodles weren't all consumed, we were all threatened with noodle sandwiches!"

---

1 cup all-purpose flour, plus extra for kneading

½ teaspoon salt

1 large egg, slightly beaten

2 tablespoons cream or whole milk

4 cups chicken broth

Salt and black pepper to taste

---

1 In a medium bowl, combine the flour and salt. Make a well in the flour, add the slightly beaten egg and cream or milk, and mix well. The dough should be stiff.

2 On a lightly floured surface, knead the dough for 3 to 4 minutes. Roll the dough out to the desired thinness. Use a knife to cut into strips of desired width. Place on parchment paper and allow to dry or until ready to use. Noodles can be used immediately.

3 When ready to serve, boil the chicken broth in a Dutch oven and drop the noodles into the pot. Reduce the heat and cook at a rolling boil for approximately 20 minutes, until the noodles are tender. Season with salt and pepper to taste. Serve hot.

MAKES 8 TO 10 SERVINGS.

INFAMOUS GIBLET GRAVY ✕✕✕

Laura Creekmore (Nashville, Tennessee) shares that as a child, every time she went to visit her grandmother, Doris Davis Norment (Whiteville, Tennessee), they cooked together. They would make fried squash, Rice Krispies treats, and lots of other dishes that appealed to Laura and her sisters. They called their grandmother DeeDee and remember her as patient and calm and a wonderful cook and teacher. Oddly enough, though, Laura shares that "DeeDee's biggest food legacy in our family is a dish I don't really like—her annual Thanksgiving giblet gravy. While my mother cooked everything else or shared in the cooking with my aunts, my cousins, and me, DeeDee made the giblet gravy as long as she was with us." DeeDee passed away in 2006.

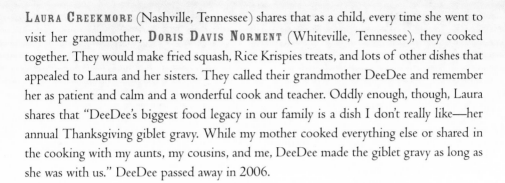

4 to 6 chicken gizzards

I teaspoon salt

2 to 4 chicken livers

1/3 cup cold water

1/4 cup all-purpose flour

4 tablespoons chicken or turkey pan drippings*

2 cups chicken broth

2 large hard-boiled eggs, chopped

Salt and black pepper to taste

1 Bring a saucepan of water to a boil; then add the gizzards and salt, and simmer for one hour. Add the livers and simmer for an additional 30 minutes. Drain, reserving pan drippings, and when cool, chop the gizzards and livers.

2 In a small bowl, slowly add cold water to the flour, mixing well.

3 In a heavy saucepan over low heat, add the pan drippings and slowly stir in the flour mixture. When well blended, slowly add the chicken broth and cook until thickened, stirring constantly. Then stir in the eggs and chopped giblets and livers. Add salt and pepper to taste before serving. Serve hot over turkey, chicken, or mashed potatoes.

MAKES 2 CUPS.

* If pan drippings are not available, use 4 tablespoons of butter or cooking oil.

GRAMMY'S CHEESE GRITS

What an amazing Grammy CATHY SANTALUCIA CLARK (Greenville, South Carolina) is! Her five grandchildren share that she loves the ocean and helps them jump the waves and find jewels, sand dollars, shells, and crabs in the sand. Each year the grandparents and their two children and spouses, who are parents to these five little ones, take a group vacation. And Grammy buys the little ones matching outfits for their annual outing to Hilton Head, South Carolina. All five of her grandchildren were born in the South—siblings MAURA and KADEN KAHUDA (Chatham, Virginia) and siblings KYLEE, JACK, and CAMERON CLARK (Ashburn, Virginia). Together, Grammy and the little ones also enjoy strawberry and blueberry picking, painting pictures, and doing crafts. And Grammy has sewn dresses and tooth pillows for these lucky grandchildren.

---

6 cups chicken broth

2 cups whole milk

1 teaspoon salt

1/2 teaspoon ground white pepper

2 cups quick-cooking grits, uncooked

1 2/3 cup (approximately 7 ounces) shredded smoked Gouda

3 tablespoons butter

---

1 Bring the chicken broth, milk, salt, and pepper to a boil in a medium pan over high heat. Gradually whisk in the grits.

2 Cover, reduce the heat to medium, and simmer 5 minutes until thickened. Add the cheese and butter and stir until melted. Serve warm.

MAKES 8 TO 10 SERVINGS.

NOTE: *Goes great with Grammy's New Orleans Shrimp on page 137.*

SARA'S SWEET POTATO CASSEROLE

JOSH EVITT (Hermitage, Tennessee) shares, "Of the many memories I have of my grand-mother, SARA WASSON SNOW (Chattanooga, Tennessee), some of the fondest are centered around Christmas. One of my family's traditions was to go to her house for Christmas dinner, which was always a special treat. She was a master of making potatoes of all types, so potatoes were always a part of the meal. To this day, I can't eat sweet potato casserole or twice-baked potatoes without thinking of her and those special times."

CASSEROLE:

4 medium sweet potatoes

1/2 cup (1 stick) butter plus additional to grease dish

2 large eggs

1 (8 ounce) package cream cheese

1 teaspoon vanilla extract

1/4 teaspoon ground cinnamon

1/4 teaspoon salt

1/2 cup sugar

TOPPING:

1 cup chopped pecans

1 cup crushed corn flakes

1/2 cup brown sugar

1 **TO MAKE THE CASSEROLE**, peel and cube the sweet potatoes and add to a large pot of boiling water. Cook until the potatoes are soft, 15 to 20 minutes.

2 In the meantime, preheat the oven to 350 degrees. Grease a 9 x 13-inch casserole dish with butter.

3 Drain the potatoes and place in a large bowl. Allow them to cool enough to touch. Mash the potatoes and add the butter, eggs, cream cheese, and vanilla. Mix well.

4 In a small bowl blend the cinnamon, salt, and sugar. Add the cinnamon mixture to the potato mixture and mix thoroughly. Spread the potato mixture into the casserole dish.

5 **TO MAKE THE TOPPING**, in a small bowl combine the pecans, corn flakes, and brown sugar and blend thoroughly. Sprinkle on top of the potato mixture. Bake for 30 minutes or until heated well through. Serve hot.

MAKES 6 TO 8 SERVINGS.

GRAMMY'S HASH BROWN CASSEROLE ✕✕✕

Siblings **WILLS**, **LIB**, and **AMELIA MCRAE** (Dothan, Alabama) share that their Grammy, **ROSALYN TIMBIE** (also of Dothan) is the ultimate hostess! Whether a simple dinner for family gatherings or a ladies' luncheon, she makes entertaining look easy. When the grandchildren visit Grammy, lots of time is spent in the kitchen helping her make things like sprinkle cookies, gingerbread houses, homemade pasta, and even crepes. Grammy's best trick for entertaining is creating her dishes ahead of time and freezing them. That way, when guests arrive she can spend her time visiting rather than slaving over the stove. While most of her menus are much fancier, the kids share that this hash brown casserole has been one of their dad's favorites for years.

I package (2 pounds) frozen hash browns, thawed

I large onion, chopped

3/4 cup (1 1/2 sticks) butter, melted, divided

I (16 ounce) container sour cream

I (10.75) can cream of mushroom soup

I cup grated Cheddar cheese

Salt and black pepper to taste

2 1/2 cups corn flakes

---

1 Preheat the oven to 350 degrees.

2 Place the potatoes in a large bowl. Add the onions and 1/2 cup of the melted butter and mix well. Add the sour cream, soup, cheese, and salt and pepper to taste.

3 In a small bowl crush the cornflakes and mix with the remaining 1/4 cup melted butter. Place the hash brown mixture in a 2 1/2- or 3-quart casserole dish. Top with the buttered corn flakes.

4 Cover and bake for 45 minutes or until heated well through.

MAKES 6 TO 8 SERVINGS.

NOTE: *Makes a great side dish for breakfast, lunch, or dinner! And it freezes well if you want to make it ahead of time.*

FRIED OKRA AND POTATOES

BRYAN CURTIS (Nashville, Tennessee) shares that his Granny, **IRENE FOSTER** (Charlotte, Tennessee), had nine children, twenty-one grandchildren, and lots of great-grandchildren. He considered himself to be one of the "lucky" grandchildren—the ones who lived in Charlotte and were able to spend the night with her during the week. He says they were lucky because Granny went to bed very early "so we could sit up and watch television or talk on the phone and do things we couldn't do that late at home. The other reason we were lucky is because we'd get a great homemade breakfast in the morning. However, by going to bed so early, Granny got up early with the chickens. She wouldn't let us 'sleep our lives away,' as she used to say."

3 cups sliced okra	1/3 cup cornmeal	1/2 teaspoon black pepper
1 1/2 cup diced raw potatoes	1/2 teaspoon salt	2/3 cup oil

1 Combine the okra, potatoes, cornmeal, salt, and pepper in a medium bowl.
2 Heat the oil in a 9- or 10-inch cast-iron skillet. Fry the mixture in the oil until the okra and potatoes are brown and tender, turning with a spatula as needed. Serve hot.

MAKES 6 TO 8 SERVINGS.

GRANDMOMMY'S CORN PUDDING

ELIZABETH WILLIS STANTON (Richmond, Virginia) came to marriage later in life for a woman of her time—she was a teacher during the Depression and would have had to quit her job to get married, shares granddaughter MARY BETH HEINE (Apex, North Carolina). Once she did marry, she began housekeeping in earnest, although her cooking efforts were not as well received in the beginning of her marriage as they later were. She once made some rock-hard pancakes that Granddaddy rolled across the floor in fun. She didn't make pancakes again until after he passed away. Known as Grandmommy, she was able to cook without a book or recipe, preferring the "a little of this and a little of that" method—especially for her delicious biscuits. Aunt Betty and her friend Kathy decided to write down the biscuit recipe in Grandmommy's later years so the family would have it. They stopped her at every step along the way to measure the ingredients and write everything down as she made them.

Vegetable shortening to prepare dish

1 (14.75 ounce) can creamed corn

3 large eggs, beaten

1/2 teaspoon nutmeg

2 rounded tablespoons cornstarch

1 heaping tablespoon sugar

1 cup milk (whole or 2 percent)

2 teaspoons butter, melted

---

1 Preheat the oven to 350 degrees. Grease a small or 1-quart casserole dish with shortening.

2 In a large bowl combine the creamed corn, eggs, nutmeg, cornstarch, sugar, and milk. Mix well. Add the butter and stir to combine.

3 Pour the mixture into the casserole dish and bake for approximately 50 minutes or until a knife inserted in the middle comes out clean.

MAKES 4 TO 6 SERVINGS.

KENTUCKY "SPOON BREAD" X X X

MARILYN HIGDON was born in Louisville, Kentucky, and now lives just across the bridge in Jeffersonville, Indiana. While Marilyn is now in her sixties, she still remembers her grandmother, BESSIE NOLIN (Franklinton, Kentucky), vividly, even though she died when Marilyn was just sixteen. Bessie was known to her grandchildren as Ma Bessie, and Marilyn has fond memories of summers spent with her on the farm where she lived with her son and his family. Ma Bessie had big upper arms, and before they'd go to sleep in her large, comfortable feather bed, Marilyn used to ask, "Can I sleep on your big fat arm tonight?" While Ma Bessie always said yes, as an adult Marilyn feels bad she called those loving arms fat. Ma Bessie continues to be remembered by so many with the tradition of a family reunion still held on that farm every year on the first Sunday in June. Even though this recipe is called spoon bread, it's actually a side dish that Ma Bessie served with fried chicken, homemade yeast rolls, and in the summer, fresh tomatoes and green beans from the garden.

Vegetable shortening to prepare dish

1 (8.75 ounce) can whole kernel corn, drained

1 (8.5 ounce) can creamed corn

1 (8.5 ounce) box yellow corn muffin mix

1 (8 ounce) container sour cream

2 large eggs, slightly beaten

1/4 cup (1/2 stick) butter, melted

2 cups shredded medium Cheddar cheese

1 Preheat the oven to 350 degrees. Grease a 2-quart casserole dish with shortening.

2 In a large bowl, stir together the two cans of corn, corn muffin mix, sour cream, eggs, and butter. Pour into the casserole dish. Bake for 40 to 45 minutes or until golden brown.

3 Top with Cheddar cheese and return to the oven for another 5 minutes or until the cheese is melted. Serve warm as a side dish.

MAKES 8 TO 10 SERVINGS.

✕✕✕ GRANA'S GROWN-UP MAC AND CHEESE

ALISON FRANCESCA COLLIER (Mount Juliet, Tennessee) was born in Stockbridge, Georgia. She is known as Grana to her seven grandchildren—LOLA, ABE, MAGGIE, and ELIZA (Lebanon, Tennessee) and ADDIE, ELENA, and CHLOE (Murfreesboro, Tennessee). According to this group of spoiled sweeties, their Grana makes up funny stories to tell them at bedtime, and they especially love having sleepovers when all seven of them get to spend the night with her and Poppy, watching movies and eating popcorn. Grana also has lots of fun crafting stuff. They make cards and other things when they're together, and they love to sing really loud to music in her car—her favorites are Elvis and Michael Jackson. And they all laugh when Grana tells Abe, yet another time, "You're my favorite grandson," and Abe always replies, "I'm your only grandson!"

Cooking spray

2 tablespoons cornstarch

I teaspoon salt

1/2 teaspoon dry mustard

1/4 teaspoon black pepper

2 1/2 cups whole milk

2 tablespoons butter

2 cups shredded sharp Cheddar cheese, divided

8 ounces elbow pasta, cooked and drained

3 tablespoons olive oil

I (10 ounce) package frozen spinach, thawed

I (6 ounce) can chopped mushrooms, drained

I (10 ounce) can diced tomatoes, drained

1 Preheat the oven to 375 degrees. Lightly spray a 2-quart casserole dish.

2 In a saucepan combine the cornstarch, salt, mustard, and pepper. Stir in the milk and butter, stirring constantly.

3 Bring to a boil over medium heat, approximately 1 minute. Remove from the heat. Stir in 1 3/4 cups of the cheese until melted. Stir in the pasta.

4 In a medium skillet over medium heat, add the olive oil and sauté the spinach, mushrooms, and tomatoes until the spinach is limp, 8 to 10 minutes. Add the sautéed vegetables to the pasta and stir to combine.

5 Spoon the pasta into the casserole dish and top with the remaining $1/4$ cup cheese. Bake uncovered for 25 minutes or until lightly browned on top.

MAKES 4 TO 6 SERVINGS.

NOTE: *Grana says her grandkids LOVE her macaroni and cheese as a meal in itself. For the grandchildren she makes it without the vegetable sauté. To make the kid-friendly version, simply follow the same directions and leave out the olive oil, spinach, mushroom, and spinach sauté.*

MAWMAW'S MAC AND CHEESE

"Close your mouth, or you're going to drink all of Lake Sinclair," ELIZABETH "LIZ" THOMAS (Milledgeville, Georgia) was known to say. She and her husband had a cabin and a huge vegetable garden on Lake Sinclair in Macon, Georgia. Liz was known to her grandchildren as MawMaw, shares granddaughter LISA BROWN MARTIN (Memphis, Tennessee), and "there was nothing like coming in from a day of boating and swimming to find that she had made her homemade macaroni and cheese along with fresh vegetables from PawPaw's garden. To 'earn our keep' we had to shell peas and shuck corn on the front porch. MawMaw always used the same oblong, deep tin pan for her macaroni and cheese—and that's the only dish she made in that pan; my mom has the pan now, and I hope to inherit it one day," Lisa adds.

Cooking spray

1 (12 ounce) package large elbow macaroni

2 tablespoons butter

1/4 cup Parmesan cheese

3 large eggs

4 cups whole milk

1/2 teaspoon salt

1 teaspoon black pepper

1 1/2 pound block Longhorn or Colby cheese, cut into thick slices

1/2 cup grated Cheddar cheese

1 Preheat the oven to 350 degrees. Lightly spray a 2 1/2-quart casserole dish.
2 Cook the macaroni per the package directions. Drain well, put back into the cooking pot, and add the butter and Parmesan cheese. Toss and set aside.
3 In a large bowl beat together the eggs, milk, salt, and pepper.
4 In the casserole dish add first a layer of macaroni, then put a layer of the slices of cheese. Repeat the layers, ending with the macaroni.
5 Pour the egg mixture over the layers. Top with the grated cheese.
6 Bake for 30 minutes or until lightly browned on top and heated well throughout. Serve hot.

MAKES 6 TO 8 SERVINGS.

MISSISSIPPI FRIED CORN X X X

JEFFRY MCGEE (Murfreesboro, Tennessee) shares that his Aunt Sarah always lived with his grandparents, and while they are long gone, he's so glad she's remained in their house. He remembers the house as always having a wonderful, distinct smell from decades of cooking and baking by his grandmother, ERMA SMITH (Tupelo, Mississippi). After visiting Aunt Sarah recently, he unpacked his bag at home and found that some of his clothes actually smelled like the house he misses. As a child, Jeffry loved Grandmother's red velvet cake so much he once asked her to make a green velvet cake the next time. He recalls her laughing and telling him she wouldn't bake a moldy-looking cake. On his list of favorite dishes would be Grandmother's chicken and dumplins, mini pecan pies, chess pie, green beans, butter beans, and homemade biscuits slathered with a pat of butter before being ladled with rich chocolate gravy. Lucky for Jeffry and his family, Aunt Sarah re-creates many of Grandmother's dishes anytime they visit.

---

4 large ears fresh corn	2 tablespoons bacon drippings	2/3 cup water
	2 tablespoons butter	Salt and black pepper to taste

---

1 Into a large bowl use the large side of a grater or a sharp knife to cut about half the thickness of the kernels off the cob. Scrape the cobs with a knife to get more of the juices out. Set the bowl aside.

2 In a large skillet over medium heat, melt the bacon drippings and butter. When melted, add the corn and stir with a wooden spoon to keep from sticking.

3 Rinse the grater with the 2/3 cup water over the skillet. If you didn't use a grater, add the 2/3 cup water directly to the skillet. Season with salt and pepper to taste.

4 Cover, reduce the heat to low, and simmer until the corn is tender, about 30 minutes, stirring continuously to avoid sticking. Add small amounts of hot water if necessary, to avoid sticking.

MAKES 4 SERVINGS.

NANNY'S POTATO PANCAKES ✕ ✕

REBECCA BARBER (Smyrna, Tennessee) remembers her Nanny, EVELYN BOSHERS (Nashville, Tennessee), as a very giving person, always helping those less fortunate. She used to say, "It only takes one person, so anyone can make a difference" and "Whatever you give will come back to you." Nanny had such a big heart and helped so many people over the years. "She has instilled in me to be giving of my time and in any other way that I can offer myself. Nanny was also a great cook, and I have fond memories of sitting at the kitchen table watching her and, as I got older, being able to help. We had such great talks. As she got older she did not cook as much, but when she did . . . mmmm, mmmm! I'll never forget those wonderful smells," Becca adds. Nanny passed away in 1986.

2 cups mashed potatoes*	6 tablespoons all-purpose flour	Salt and black pepper to taste
I large egg, beaten lightly	1/4 cup grated onion	I tablespoon vegetable oil
	2 tablespoons chopped chives	

1 In a large bowl combine the potatoes, egg, flour, onion, chives, salt, and pepper. Mix well.

2 In a large nonstick skillet, heat the oil over medium-high heat. Drop the potato mixture by large spoonfuls into the hot oil, and flatten each with the back of a spoon or spatula. Fry approximately 2 minutes or until golden brown on each side. Remove from the skillet and blot off any excess oil on paper towels before serving. Serve hot as a side dish with breakfast, lunch, or dinner.

MAKES 4 TO 6 SERVINGS.

* Leftover mashed potatoes are perfect for this recipe.

✕✕✕ IDA'S PIMENTO SQUASH CASSEROLE

KRISTI HANCOCK (Mount Juliet, Tennessee) shares, "My grandmother—MARTHA WILLIAMS WHITLEY (Nashville, Tennessee)—has the sweetest, old-fashioned Southern accent. She truly sounds like a modern-day Scarlett O'Hara. Every time I see her, the first thing that comes out of her mouth is 'Well, hi, dahlin.' My sister and I used to love going over to her house because we knew we would get to play dress up. We each had our own bag of clothes to play with, and she would save us her little samples of Avon lipstick to 'try.' While Granny Martha is an excellent cook, my most favorite memory growing up was the little bowls of colored Jell-O with whipped cream that she'd have waiting for my sister and me whenever she knew we were coming for a visit." Granny Martha makes this casserole that's become a family favorite. The recipe was handed down from her mother, Kristi's, great-great-grandmother, Ida Hite Williams.

2 cups yellow summer squash, cooked

1 medium onion, chopped

1 (10.75) can cream of chicken soup

2 medium carrots, grated

1 (4 ounce) jar diced pimentos, drained

1 (8 ounce) container sour cream

Salt and black pepper to taste

½ cup (1 stick) butter

1 (14 ounce) package herb seasoned stuffing mix, divided

1 Preheat the oven to 350 degrees.
2 In a large saucepan boil the squash and onion until tender. Drain and mash with a fork. Add the soup, carrots, pimentos, and sour cream. Season with salt and pepper to taste.
3 In a 9 x 13-inch casserole dish, melt the butter in the oven. Remove from the oven and stir half of the stuffing into the melted butter to line the bottom of the casserole dish. Spoon the squash mixture on top of the buttered stuffing. Cover the top with the remaining stuffing. Bake for 30 minutes or until heated well through.

MAKES 8 SERVINGS.

B. G.'S BBC'S (A.K.A. BUTTERED BALSAMIC CARROTS)

GRAYSON BUTTERS (Brentwood, Tennessee) calls his grandma B. G.—BETTY KEELING GREEN WOOTEN (Nashville, Tennessee). Grayson absolutely loves to visit B. G. at her historic home in East Nashville, where she lives with her husband Big Jim, Dolly the Doberman, Lucy the cat, and Skeeter the crazy Westie. B. G. and Grayson share a love of animals (and garden-fresh veggies). When Grayson visits B. G.'s house, there is no shortage of treats on hand—from homemade ice cream to fresh-baked cookies. Sometimes, despite his mommy's rules, B. G. even serves ice cream for dinner. And, of course, Grayson loves to hand out doggie treats to Skeeter and Dolly for dessert!

1 pound carrots	1 tablespoon maple syrup	1/8 teaspoon salt
1 tablespoon butter	1 teaspoon balsamic vinegar	1/8 teaspoon black pepper

1 Peel and slice carrots in 1/4-inch slices. Place the carrots in a saucepan, cover, and steam them for about 15 minutes, until thoroughly cooked but not mushy.

2 Melt the butter in a medium skillet over medium heat. (Make sure the skillet is big enough to hold the carrots once the sauce is completed.) Cook the butter (stirring occasionally) for about 3 minutes or until it gets a bit brown.

3 Stir in the syrup, vinegar, salt, and pepper. Add the carrots, stir to coat them in the sauce, and cook until heated through.

MAKES 4 SERVINGS.

K. K.'S RUMMY SWEET POTATO APPLE BAKE

KATHERINE CORTNER KEELING (Nashville, Tennessee) is known as K. K. to her three grandchildren and Great K. K. to her six great-grandchildren. Her oldest granddaughter, MANDY BUTTERS (Brentwood, Tennessee), remembers K. K. "putting up" creamed corn—dozens and dozens of ears, using the tip and scrape method (cut off the tips of the kernels; then scrape the knife down the side to get the pulp and juice off the cob). "There would be corn pieces and juice everywhere—on the walls, windows, floor, etc.," Mandy recalls. And though the end is broken off and the blade has practically all been filed away, K. K. still has (and uses as her favorite) the knife she got on her wedding day, seventy-some years ago.

---

3 pounds sweet potatoes

Butter to grease dish

3 medium Golden Delicious apples

1/4 cup fresh lemon juice

I cup pecan halves

8 tablespoons butter

1/2 cup firmly packed light brown sugar

1/2 cup honey

2 tablespoons dark rum

1/4 teaspoon ground ginger

1/4 teaspoon ground mace

1/2 teaspoon ground cinnamon

---

1 Wash the sweet potatoes and prick each several times with a fork. In a large casserole dish or roaster, bake the sweet potatoes until tender, approximately 45 minutes. Cool and peel the potatoes. Cut crosswise into 1/4-inch slices and place in a buttered 9 x 13-inch baking pan.

2 Preheat the oven to 400 degrees.

3 Peel, core, and slice the apples lengthwise. Toss them in lemon juice. Add the apples to the casserole dish with the sweet potatoes. Sprinkle with pecan halves.

4 In a medium saucepan over medium heat, combine the butter, brown sugar, honey, rum, ginger, mace, and cinnamon. Cook the mixture until the sugar dissolves, stirring constantly.

5 Pour the mixture over the sweet potatoes and apples in the casserole dish. Bake for 30 minutes. Baste occasionally with the butter sauce.

6 After 30 minutes, place the casserole dish under the broiler, just until the edges of the sweet potatoes and apples are slightly browned. Serve warm.

MAKES 8 TO 10 SERVINGS.

NOTE: *Careful with the rum—adding too much may cause a fire in the oven, Just ask K. K.! She made that mistake once . . .*

MAMA DEE'S CHRISTMAS DRESSING

Grandmother DOLORES LILLIAN WADE SIMPSON (Fort Smith, Arkansas) makes the absolute best dressing, shares granddaughter AUDRA EBERMAN WARZYNSKI (also of Fort Smith), and the holidays would just not be complete without it. Audra's grandfather, Daddy Jim, is the official taste-tester, and she says, "Each year, in effort to achieve perfection with his wife's Christmas Dressing, he says, 'Mama, I think this is the best ever'—and, bless his eighty-eight-year-old heart, he is always right." Three tables are now required for their large family, with each place setting decorated with a personalized ornament, making everyone feel special. Dolores is known to her grandchildren as Mama Dee.

1/2 cup bacon drippings or butter

6 medium onions, chopped

12 cups chopped celery

10 cups white bread crumbs, dried

12 cups cornbread, crumbled

6 heaping teaspoons rubbed sage seasoning or poultry seasoning

Salt and black pepper to taste

5 large eggs, beaten

1/4 cup turkey drippings

2 cups chicken broth*

1 Preheat the oven to 400 degrees.

2 In a large skillet over medium heat, melt the bacon drippings. Add the onion and celery and sauté until tender.

3 In a large bowl combine the bread crumbs, cornbread, sage, salt, and pepper. Add the sautéed onions and celery to the bread mixture.

4 Add the eggs and turkey drippings and carefully stir to combine. Begin adding the chicken broth a small amount at a time. Use additional as needed to make the dressing the same consistency as a cornbread batter, moist but not soupy. Spoon into a large roaster or disposable foil pan (18.5 x 14 inches or similar).

5 Bake for 30 minutes or until a toothpick stuck in the dressing comes out clean; stir at least once during baking.

MAKES 15 TO 20 SERVINGS.

* Or use water mixed with melted butter to make two cups of liquid.

NOTE: *Old breads tend to soak up more liquid than fresh bread, so fold in the liquid a little at a time to get the right consistency.*

Ham and Cheese Rolls

Chicken and Dumplings

Old Mommie's Chicken Divan
    Casserole

Stuffed Peppers

Louisiana Shrimp Boil

Mammy's Southern Fried
    Chicken and Cream Gravy

Nutty Oven-Fried Chicken

Summer Tomato Pie

Mom Mom's Meat Loaf

Grammy's New Orleans Shrimp

Nana's Biggie Chicken

Turkey Crunch Casserole

Honey Lou's Poppy Seed Chicken

Granny Spaghetti

Stroganoff à la Oma

Gran's Golden Chicken Nuggets

Mammy's Rio Grande Roast

Nanny's Tollerine

Chicken and Doop

Mama Kee's Chicken Royale

Vallie's Supper-Quick Casserole

Betty's Hot Dog Chili

Granddaddy's Favorite Casserole

Froggy More Stew

Skillet Fried Chicken

Grammy's Hot Chicken Salad
    Casserole

Main Dishes

✕✕✕ HAM AND CHEESE ROLLS

LARISSA ARNAULT (Nashville, Tennessee) is originally from Searcy, Arkansas. Her Mamaw Lucy was LUCY HARRIS of Weir, Mississippi. Larissa shares that "Mamaw Lucy was certainly the matriarch of our family, as many Southern grandmothers are. I would go to her house in the morning, and before I left that afternoon, she had made my doll a detailed dress, complete with smocking. She took time to do things that mattered the right way, but she didn't waste time being extravagant for no reason. I also remember all of the women of our family (four generations) gathering around her TV each day for lunch to watch *Days of Our Lives*. Mamaw Lucy was a spiritual influence as well, and I vividly remember a print that hung in her kitchen called *Daily Bread* of a man praying at the dinner table." Larissa adds that they always had these rolls at holidays, made with ham that was left over from the main meal.

I cup (2 sticks) butter

3 tablespoons prepared mustard

3 tablespoons poppy seeds

I medium onion, finely chopped

I teaspoon Worcestershire sauce

2 packages (12 rolls in each) dinner rolls in tin pans

6 square slices Swiss cheese (quartered to make 24 small squares)

6 square slices pasteurized processed cheese, Cheddar, or American cheese (quartered to make 24 small squares)

24 pieces thinly sliced ham (folded into 2 x 2-inch pieces)

---

1 Preheat the oven to 400 degrees.
2 In a medium skillet, melt the butter. Then add the mustard, poppy seeds, onion, and Worcestershire sauce. Simmer on low to medium heat until the onion is transparent.
3 Remove the dinner rolls from the pan as one sheet and slice, placing the bottom half back into the tin pan they came in. Spread the mustard mixture on the rolls and layer the cheese slices and ham on top. Place the top sheet of the rolls on top and cover with foil.
4 Place in the oven and bake for 15 to 20 minutes until the cheese is melted and the rolls are heated through. Serve warm.

MAKES 24 SERVINGS.

SHERON DUGAN TYGRET (Mount Juliet, Tennessee) learned a strong work ethic from her grandmother, SARAH FRANCES PEWITT (Franklin, Tennessee). This chicken and dumplings recipe has become one of her family's favorites, and Sheron says she can't ever make enough of it for her three sons. Sheron has fond memories of big lunch get-togethers on Sundays with Grandmother's seven children and their families. "I remember going to the henhouse with Grandmother and watching in awe as she bravely put her hand under the hens and retrieved their eggs. And Grandmother made the best biscuits I've ever had in my life. She'd make them at lunch (the big meal of the day on the farm) and put the leftovers on a plate in the gas oven, where they stayed soft until they were eaten at dinner," Sheron adds. Her grandmother passed away in 1978.

I hen or large chicken fryer	4 cups all-purpose flour	Black pepper and additional salt to taste
I teaspoon salt, divided	3/4 cup vegetable shortening	

---

1 Place the chicken in a 4-quart Dutch oven and cover with water. Bring to a boil. Add 1/2 teaspoon of the salt and reduce the heat to medium-low and allow to simmer I to 2 hours (until the chicken is falling off the bones).

2 Remove the chicken from the pot and allow to cool. Do not discard the broth. Debone the chicken and cut into bite-size pieces. Set the chicken aside.

3 In a large bowl add the flour and remaining 1/2 teaspoon salt. Cut the shortening into the flour thoroughly with a pastry blender. Add enough broth from the cooked chicken (about I 1/2 cups) to make a stiff dough. Roll the dough to about 1/8 inch thick and cut into strips about 4 inches long.

4 Bring the remaining broth in the Dutch oven to a boil. Drop the dough strips into the boiling broth; then reduce the heat to medium-low. Add black pepper and additional salt to taste and simmer for 20 minutes. Add the chicken and stir slowly until heated through. Serve hot in bowls.

MAKES 8 SERVINGS.

OLD MOMMIE'S CHICKEN DIVAN CASSEROLE

CAROL ANN RUPP CRAWLEY (Alton, Virginia) was actually born in Punxsutawney, Pennsylvania. This mother of five is known as Old Mommie to her nine grandchildren, seven of whom were born in the South. (The other two were born and are being raised in Japan.) Granddaughter BRETT MAYLNN SEATE was born in Jacksonville, North Carolina, and has lived in Virginia, Tennessee, and Washington State. When they were younger and visiting, Brett and her older sister, Selena, liked to ride in the back of their grandfather Ampy's pickup truck around the farm and through the woods. The girls also liked to dress up in the play clothes kept in a special dress-up box and perform for the rest of the family. Old Mommie's chicken divan is always a hit, and people especially enjoy the taste of her "secret" ingredient . . . curry.

Cooking spray

4 large chicken breasts, cooked

2 (10 ounce) packages frozen chopped broccoli

1 cup grated Cheddar cheese

1 cup mayonnaise

2 (14.25 ounce) cans cream of chicken soup

1 teaspoon curry powder

1 cup bread crumbs

3 tablespoons margarine

---

1 Preheat the oven to 350 degrees. Spray the bottom and sides of a 9 x 13-inch casserole dish.

2 Shred the cooked chicken and place in the bottom of the casserole dish. Steam the broccoli according to the package directions, drain, and place on top of the shredded chicken in the casserole dish.

3 In a medium bowl mix together the cheese, mayonnaise, cream of chicken soup, and curry powder.

4 Pour the mixture on top of the broccoli. Sprinkle the bread crumbs and then small pieces of the margarine over the soup mixture and bake for 25 to 30 minutes until bubbly and heated well through.

MAKES 6 TO 8 SERVINGS.

ELIZABETH "LIB" BOWMAN HAUSER (Liberty, North Carolina) named two of her three children—Beth and Bryan—for her Grandma Mac, ALIVIE ELIZABETH BRYAN McPHERSON (Liberty, North Carolina). Lib has fond memories of making homemade sausage and pork rinds with her Grandma Mac as well as canning tomato juice. Lib says everything was canned because they didn't have a freezer until she was ten years old. They also sliced and dried their apples to enjoy as a snack during the winter months. Lib shares they always had a garden in the summer and often had too many peppers ripe at the same time. This recipe is a great way to use all the peppers and freeze some for future meals.

6 medium green bell peppers, whole

1 pound ground beef

1 teaspoon salt (optional)

$^1/_4$ teaspoon black pepper

1 cup cracker crumbs, crushed

1 tablespoon chopped onion

1 (10.5 ounce) can tomato soup, divided

5 $^1/_4$ ounces water

1 Preheat the oven to 350 degrees.

2 In a medium pot boil enough water to immerse the green peppers whole. Once the water boils, place the whole peppers in the pot and boil, uncovered, for 5 minutes. Drain the peppers and let them cool.

3 In a large bowl combine the ground beef, salt, pepper, cracker crumbs, onion, and half of the tomato soup. Mix well.

4 Remove the stems and insides of the cooled green peppers. Stuff each pepper with the meat mixture and place upright in a glass casserole dish or a small roaster.

5 Add the water to the remaining soup (just pour it right into the can). Stir the water and soup and pour on top of the stuffed peppers.

6 Cover and bake for 50 to 60 minutes. Uncover during the last 10 minutes of baking. Serve warm.

MAKES 6 SERVINGS.

LOUISIANA SHRIMP BOIL ✕✕✕

While **CHRISTINE KARCHER** currently lives in Nashville, Tennessee, she was born in England and raised in Shreveport, Louisiana. Christine is affectionately known as Mimi or Grana to her two granddaughters, Zivah and Divya. **ZIVAH RENEE KARCHER** (Nashville, Tennessee) is the firstborn grandchild, and Christine loves the crayon drawings she has from her. Together, Grana and her husband (Grandpa) and the girls' parents run a video and photography business. So, as you can imagine, they have many beautiful images of the girls they all treasure. Christine looks forward to sharing family traditions and recipes with the girls as they grow up.

---

8 quarts water

6 whole cloves garlic, chopped

4 lemons, halved

2 large onions, chopped coarsely

1 stalk celery, chopped coarsely

2 bay leaves

1 bag crab boil spice pack

$1/2$ teaspoon salt

1 teaspoon cayenne pepper

2 pounds new potatoes, scrubbed

4 ears corn, cut in half

2 pounds shell-on shrimp, deveined, head removed

4 tablespoons butter

---

1 In a large pot, add the water, garlic, lemons, onions, celery, bay leaves, crab boil, salt, and cayenne pepper. Bring to a boil and let simmer for about 5 minutes.

2 Add the potatoes and let the water come back to a boil. Cook for about 8 minutes; then add the corn and continue to boil until the potatoes and corn are almost done.

3 Add the shrimp, return to a boil, and cook for 4 minutes or until shrimp are pink. Turn off the burner and let stand for 8 minutes.

4 Test seasoning for your taste preference. If not seasoned enough, add more salt and cayenne pepper.

5 Remove shrimp, potatoes, and corn. Discard all of the broth except for 2 cups.

6 Strain the broth and add it to a medium skillet with the butter. Heat on low until the butter melts and the mixture is well blended. Pour the broth and butter mixture over the shrimp, potatoes, and corn. Serve warm.

MAKES 8 SERVINGS.

MAMMY'S SOUTHERN FRIED CHICKEN AND CREAM GRAVY

Mammy, LUCY ADAMS REYNOLDS (Springfield, Tennessee), had a good sense of humor and had no problem laughing at herself. She also loved unconditionally, remembers her granddaughter, WANDA WATTS (also of Springfield). "I hope that I learned those things from her. Mammy's favorite saying was related to children misbehaving. In observance of such behavior, she'd point them out to me and say, 'She's a ring-tail-tooter.'" Wanda also shares, "I could be a princess to all those around me, but when life handed me difficult times and others depended on me, Mammy knew I would be able to step up to the challenge. She knew me better than I knew myself." Mammy passed away in 1973.

SOUTHERN FRIED CHICKEN:

1 large fryer cut into pieces

1/2 cup all-purpose flour, sifted

1/2 teaspoon salt

1/8 teaspoon black pepper

1 large egg, slightly beaten

1/3 cup buttermilk

Lard or vegetable oil for frying

CHICKEN CREAM GRAVY:

4 tablespoons pan drippings from fried chicken

4 tablespoons flour

2 cups chicken broth

1/4 cup evaporated milk

Salt and black pepper to taste

1 **TO MAKE THE CHICKEN**, rinse the chicken pieces and wipe dry.

2 In a large bowl combine the flour with the salt and pepper. Combine the beaten egg and buttermilk in a small bowl and stir into the flour mixture. Mix well.

3 Melt the lard or pour vegetable oil about 1 inch deep in a large skillet with a lid. When the lard or oil reaches 350 degrees, dip the chicken pieces into the batter and carefully place the chicken pieces into the skillet. Allow to brown and then cover the pan, reduce heat to medium, and allow to cook slowly until tender, 30 to 35 minutes.

4 Remove from the oil and keep warm on a wire rack in the oven. Serve with Chicken Cream Gravy.

5 To MAKE THE GRAVY, heat the pan drippings over medium heat. Add the flour and whisk until smooth. Slowly stir the chicken broth into the flour mixture, whisking constantly, until the gravy is smooth and boiling. Slowly add the evaporated milk. Season to taste with salt and pepper.

MAKES 6 SERVINGS.

NUTTY OVEN-FRIED CHICKEN ✕ ✕ ✕

PATSY CANNON (Greenville, South Carolina) enjoys cooking for her family and has quite the green thumb. She loves working in her garden, and grandson, WELLS GREER CANNON (born in Nashville, Tennessee, and now living in Colorado), enjoys exploring her garden and backyard when he's in South Carolina for a visit. Wells loves taking airplane trips to South Carolina to visit his Nanny and Papa and shares, "Nanny spoils me when I visit, always having presents for me, giving me fun treats, and, of course, lots of her special hugs and cuddles. One of my favorite things to do with Nanny when I visit is to read books with her before my bedtime."

Cooking spray

I cup biscuit mix

2 teaspoons salt

$1/2$ teaspoon poultry seasoning

$1/2$ teaspoon sage

$1/3$ cup pecans, finely chopped

I (2 $1/2$ to 3 pound) chicken, cut up

$1/2$ cup evaporated milk

$1/2$ cup (I stick) butter, melted

1 Preheat the oven to 350 degrees. Lightly spray a 13 x 9 x 2-inch baking pan.

2 Combine the biscuit mix, salt, poultry seasoning, sage, and pecans in a bowl.

3 Dip the chicken pieces in the evaporated milk; then coat generously with the pecan mixture. Place in the baking pan. Poor the melted butter over the chicken. Bake for approximately I hour or until the chicken is cooked through.

MAKES 4 SERVINGS.

SUMMER TOMATO PIE ✕ ✕ ✕

DIANE HOOKER CALLAHAN was born in Huntsville, Alabama, and currently lives in Nashville, Tennessee. Her Granny, ETHEL HOOKER (Eads, Tennessee), had eight grandchildren and lived to be 101 years old. Diane remembers her as a very smart and loving lady. "I have really fond memories of visiting my Granny and Granddad for a couple of weeks each summer and staying on their farm. We would pick fresh tomatoes and vegetables every day from their garden, and this recipe is one Granny used when the garden was overflowing with tomatoes. The smell and taste of fresh tomatoes was addictive, and all I wanted to eat was tomatoes with saltines. (Now, that's Southern!) I think this tomato pie may have been her way to get some variety into my meals, and it worked," Diane adds.

4 large tomatoes

1 cup shredded sharp Cheddar cheese, divided

1 (9-inch) piecrust, baked

1/2 cup chopped green onion

12 fresh basil leaves, chopped

Salt and black pepper to taste

1/3 cup mayonnaise

1 Preheat the oven to 350 degrees.
2 Blanch the tomatoes in a pot of boiling water for 20 seconds. Immediately place them into some cold water so the skin will peel off much easier. Peel the tomatoes, salt to taste, and let drain in a colander for 20 minutes. Pat with paper towels to remove most of the moisture. Then cut them into slices.
3 Layer 1/3 cup of the cheese in the bottom of the piecrust. Layer slices of the tomato on top of the cheese. Sprinkle the green onions and basil on top of the tomato slices. Salt and pepper to your taste.
4 In a small bowl mix the mayonnaise and remaining cheese together and layer on top of the pie. Bake for 25 to 30 minutes. Let cool at least 15 minutes before slicing.

MAKES 8 SERVINGS.

MOM MOM'S MEAT LOAF

JESSICA HENDERSON (Franklin, Tennessee) shares that her Mom Mom, CAROLYN BOOTH (Nashville, Tennessee), has taught her the importance of being classy. "I really admire her Southern charm and how well she carries herself. She has taught me manners, how to act in public, and how to have self-respect and respect for others. She has shown me how to be a strong woman, how to love your family and husband well, and how to treat other people. Mom Mom has also taught me how to plant myself firm in my faith and how to love God. She's a great Christian woman, and I hope I can be like her when I am a grandmother," Jessica says.

MEAT LOAF:

Cooking spray

2 pounds ground round

1 cup bread crumbs

2 large eggs

3/4 cup ketchup

1 teaspoon salt substitute

1/2 cup warm water

1 (1 ounce) envelope onion soup mix

TOPPING:

1 (8 ounce) can tomato sauce

1/2 cup sugar

2 tablespoons brown sugar

2 teaspoons prepared mustard

2 tablespoons vinegar

1 Preheat the oven to 350 degrees. Lightly spray a 5 x 9-inch loaf pan.

2 TO MAKE THE MEAT LOAF, in a large bowl mix the ground round and bread crumbs.

3 In a small bowl beat the eggs; add the ketchup, salt substitute, warm water, and soup mix and blend well. Pour the soup mixture into the meat and mix well. Shape the meat into the loaf pan. Bake for 45 minutes.

4 TO MAKE THE TOPPING, in a small bowl mix together the tomato sauce, sugar, brown sugar, mustard, and vinegar and pour over the meat loaf. Bake for an additional 15 minutes.

5 Remove from the oven. Pour off any excess grease. Allow to cool for 10 to 15 minutes before slicing.

MAKES 8 TO 10 SERVINGS.

NOTE: You can also roll meat loaf into balls and bake in a muffin tin. Place a cookie sheet under to catch grease. After baking for 45 minutes, transfer the balls to a casserole dish, add the topping, and bake for an additional 15 minutes.

GRAMMY'S NEW ORLEANS SHRIMP ✕✕✕

CATHY SANTALUCIA CLARK (Greenville, South Carolina) was born in Pennsylvania, but she's lived much of her adult life in the South: fourteen years in Atlanta, Georgia; six years in Florida; four years in Richmond, Virginia; and one year in South Carolina. Cathy is a mother of two and a grandmother to five. She is known as Grammy to her grandchildren, all of whom were born in the South: MAURA and KADEN KAHUDA were born in Chatham, Virginia, and KYLEE, JACK, and CAMERON CLARK were all born in Ashburn, Virginia. When Cathy's children were little and they lived in Atlanta, they would go to St. Simon's Island on vacation with two other families. They always had this shrimp one night since it is easy to prepare and everyone could eat their fill. They could be as messy as they wanted, peeling the shrimp and sopping up the sauce with bread. Grammy now carries on the tradition every year in Hilton Head with the whole family. "We always have this dish one night and then do a low-country boil another night later in the week. My grandchildren are a little too young to appreciate it yet, but I know they will one day soon. For now we just order them pizza," she says.

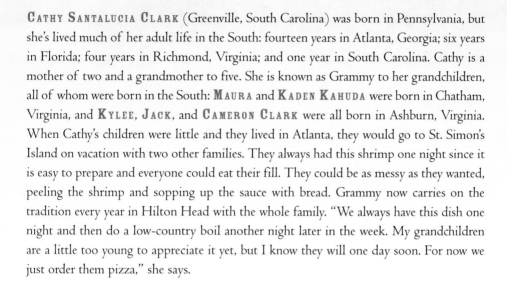

I cup butter

I cup olive oil

I (16 ounce) bottle Italian salad dressing

I 1/2 tablespoons black pepper

I 1/2 tablespoons salt

I clove garlic, pressed

1/2 cup vermouth

3/4 tablespoon cayenne pepper

3/4 tablespoon paprika

I medium onion, chopped

5 pounds medium shrimp in shell, uncooked

---

1 In a Dutch oven over medium heat, melt the butter, then add the oil, salad dressing, black pepper, salt, garlic, vermouth, cayenne pepper, paprika, and onion. Simmer for 20 minutes.

2 Place the uncooked shrimp in a large casserole dish. Pour the cooked sauce over the shrimp. Bake 25 to 30 minutes, stirring occasionally.

MAKES 10 SERVINGS.

NOTE: *Cathy suggests serving with chopped salad and French bread for sopping up the sauce. She adds that it serves an army and leftovers are really good too!*

NANA'S BIGGIE CHICKEN

While originally from Lothian, Maryland, JANE ANN GRAHAM (Murfreesboro, Tennessee) has lived in the South since 1991. Grandson JOSHUA ASHTON GRAHAM (also of Murfreesboro) shares that his Nana is the prettiest, kindest, and most generous person in the world. She loves to travel and on a dime will go anywhere! He says that "our birthdays are one day apart, and we celebrate together every year. We also share the same initials (J.A.G.), and together we like to read *I Spy* books, make blueberry muffins, and have movie nights. She's always taught me to say, 'I love you' before bed, and I especially love her spaghetti and, of course, this biggie chicken." He also adds that his mom doesn't cook much, so he hopes that Nana will teach her!

2 (16 ounce) containers sour cream

1/4 cup lemon juice

2 teaspoons Worcestershire sauce

2 teaspoons paprika

2 garlic cloves, pressed

Salt and black pepper to taste

6 to 8 boneless, skinless chicken breasts

1 3/4 cups seasoned bread crumbs

1/2 cup (1 stick) butter

1 In a large bowl combine the sour cream, lemon juice, Worcestershire sauce, paprika, garlic, salt, and pepper. Coat each piece of chicken in the mixture and place in a shallow casserole dish in a single layer. Let stand covered overnight in the refrigerator.

2 When ready to bake the next day, preheat the oven to 350 degrees.

3 Roll the chicken in the bread crumbs and place back in the shallow casserole dish. Melt the butter and spoon it over each piece of chicken.

4 Bake uncovered for approximately 50 minutes or until the chicken is tender and lightly browned.

MAKES 6 TO 8 SERVINGS.

TURKEY CRUNCH CASSEROLE ✕ ✕ ✕

"Well, flitter!" (instead of, "Well, shoot!") this grandma used to say. Known to her grandchildren as Granny, VIVIAN LOVORN was born and raised in Union, Mississippi. She loved to cook and have family and friends over to eat. Granddaughter KATHY SPEARS (Franklin, Tennessee) shares that "Granny was always prim and proper, dressing to the nines anytime she went anywhere—even to the mailbox! I learned manners from her, and she never met a stranger, which is probably why I'm quite sociable. She also inspired my love of cooking."

3 cups diced turkey (or chicken)

2 large hard-boiled eggs, chopped

1 (4 ounce) can sliced mushrooms

3/4 cup diced celery

1 tablespoon chopped onion

1 (10.75 ounce) can cream of mushroom soup

3/4 cup mayonnaise

1 3/4 cups hard chow mein noodles or crushed potato chips

1 Preheat the oven to 350 degrees.

2 In a large bowl mix together the turkey, eggs, mushrooms, celery, and onion. In a small bowl stir the soup into the mayonnaise and toss with the turkey mixture. Spoon the mixture into a 2-quart casserole dish.

3 Top with the chow mein noodles. Bake for 30 minutes or until bubbling and heated well through.

MAKES 6 TO 8 SERVINGS.

✕✕✕ HONEY LOU'S POPPY SEED CHICKEN

Every Easter morning following church, CAROLINE RAY (Memphis, Tennessee) and her family would pack into their minivan and head to Shelbyville, Tennessee, to celebrate the holiday with Granddaddy and Grandma, HONEY LOU GLASSCOCK. Caroline shares, "Like most children, for me the anticipation the night before Easter was high. Yes, I was excited to see what goodies the Easter bunny would leave in my basket, but most of all, I could not wait for Grandma Honey Lou's Southern cooking. Easter dinner has always lived up to the hype: sweet tea, honey-baked ham, the most delicious sides to accompany the meal, and my favorite: Honey Lou's poppy seed chicken! The creamy chicken with a hint of sour cream and cheese and the crunch from the butter crackers topping make for the perfect comfort food. After we gather around the kitchen table and say, 'Bless Us, O Lord' in unison, being the sweet Southern hostess she is, Grandma always insists that we fix our plates before she does. We split off into our respective tables, adults and kids, and rave about our overflowing plates. Although Easter gatherings have changed throughout the years from Easter egg hunts and jelly beans to adult grandchildren reminiscing on the porch swing while enjoying homemade banana pudding, Grandma's ability to 'wow' us with her Southern cuisine has remained a constant."

CHICKEN DISH:

Vegetable shortening to prepare pan

1 (10.75 ounce) can cream of chicken soup

1 (10.75 ounce) can cream of celery soup

1 (8 ounce) container sour cream

2 tablespoons poppy seeds

1 sleeve round butter crackers, crumbled

5 chicken breasts, cooked and cut up

TOPPING:

1 sleeve round butter crackers, crumbled

1 tablespoon poppy seeds

½ cup (1 stick) butter, melted

1   Preheat the oven to 350 degrees. Grease a 9 x 13-inch baking pan.
2   TO MAKE THE CHICKEN DISH, in a medium bowl combine the creamed soups, sour cream, and poppy seeds and mix well. Add the crumbled crackers and cut-up chicken. Mix well and place in the casserole dish.

3 To **MAKE THE TOPPING**, in a small bowl combine the crumbled crackers and poppy seeds and mix well. Spoon on top of the chicken mixture. Drizzle the melted butter on top. Bake for 30 minutes and serve warm.

MAKES 8 SERVINGS.

GRANNY SPAGHETTI ✗✗

IRENE FOSTER was born, raised, and lived all her life in Charlotte, Tennessee. She was a mother of nine and grandmother to twenty-one, who affectionately called her Granny. Grandson **BRYAN CURTIS** (Nashville, Tennessee) recalls that he and his grandmother shared a love of the soap opera *All My Children*. Growing up before there were VCRs or DVRs, if he didn't catch an episode, Bryan would call Granny to catch up on any scoop he missed. Bryan says he wishes he had a dollar for every time she said, "That Erica Kane." If you have it, Bryan says the secret to this recipe is using home-canned tomato juice, like Granny did. Her family always tried to re-create this dish, and it affectionately became known as Granny Spaghetti.

1/4 cup bacon drippings	8 ounces spaghetti, cooked according to package directions	4 cups tomato juice
1/2 cup finely chopped onion		1/2 teaspoon salt
		1/2 teaspoon black pepper

1 Add the bacon drippings to a large saucepan and place over medium heat. Add the onion and sauté until tender. Add the cooked and drained spaghetti, tomato juice, salt, and pepper. Bring to a boil and simmer for 8 to 10 minutes.

MAKES 8 SERVINGS.

NOTE: *Granny would serve this with white beans, slaw, and cornbread.*

STROGANOFF À LA OMA ✕ ✕

Grandmother **DIANNE MARIE EILAND HEGLER** (Williamsport, Tennessee) was raised in Opp, Alabama. She is known as Oma to her two young granddaughters. **ELLA ANNELISE HEGLER'S** (Mount Juliet, Tennessee) mom, Marie Hegler, says that when Ella is old enough, she will be learning her way around the kitchen with Oma, just like Marie did. Oma has always has been adventurous in the kitchen, taking recipes and putting her spin on them to make them her own. Because of her husband's military career, she moved around a lot and was introduced to many different styles of cooking and a wide range of ingredients. (Her husband is a retired US Air Force colonel.) Marie shares, "Our family was always willing to try out her new recipes, and rarely did Mom make a dish that we didn't enjoy, though we all had our favorites. One of those favorites was this stroganoff that we usually ate over rice or sometimes just on top of toast."

1 small onion, diced

1 (4.5 ounce) jar mushrooms, drained, or 1 cup chopped fresh mushrooms

2 tablespoons butter

2 tablespoons olive oil

1 pound ground beef

1/2 teaspoon garlic powder

Salt and black pepper to taste

1 (8 ounce) can sliced water chestnuts, drained

1 (14.25 ounce) can cream of chicken soup

1 (8 ounce) container sour cream

1 In a large skillet over medium heat, sauté the onion and mushrooms (if fresh) in the butter and olive oil. Remove from the pan.

2 Add the ground beef to the skillet and brown. Drain off the excess grease; add the garlic powder and salt and pepper to taste.

3 Add back in the onions and mushrooms; stir in the water chestnuts and soup. Simmer for 5 minutes, covered.

4 Turn off the heat, stir in the sour cream, and serve. This is delicious served over rice or egg noodles or on top of toast.

MAKES 4 TO 6 SERVINGS.

GRAN'S GOLDEN CHICKEN NUGGETS

CADE BENTLEY HAMPTON (Mount Juliet, Tennessee) and his sister love to visit and vacation with their Pop and Gran, SHERRY BOND HAMPTON (Caddo, Alabama). The Hampton kids come from a long line of Alabama fans, and these nuggets are perfect for tailgating or watching a weekend game with Gran and Pop. These homemade chicken nuggets were Cade's dad's and his Uncle Jamey's favorites when they were little boys, and they still act like little boys when she makes them today. Cade adds, "We all love these nuggets and fight over the crumbs left on the paper towel when the plate is empty."

Vegetable or peanut oil for frying

1 large egg, beaten

3/4 teaspoon salt

1/2 cup water

1/2 cup all-purpose flour

3 chicken breasts (boned, skinned, and cut into small pieces)

1   Fill a large Dutch oven with approximately 3 inches of oil. Heat the oil to 350 degrees.

2   In a shallow bowl mix together the egg, salt, water, and flour. Dip the chicken pieces into the batter to fully coat.

3   Cook a few pieces at a time in the oil for approximately 3 minutes on each side. Remove from the grease and blot on paper towels before serving. Serve hot.

MAKES 3 TO 5 SERVINGS.

MAMMY'S RIO GRANDE ROAST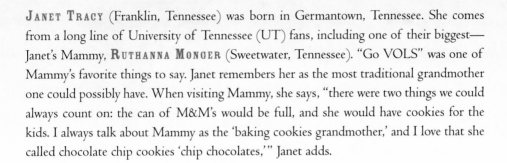

JANET TRACY (Franklin, Tennessee) was born in Germantown, Tennessee. She comes from a long line of University of Tennessee (UT) fans, including one of their biggest—Janet's Mammy, RUTHANNA MONGER (Sweetwater, Tennessee). "Go VOLS" was one of Mammy's favorite things to say. Janet remembers her as the most traditional grandmother one could possibly have. When visiting Mammy, she says, "there were two things we could always count on: the can of M&M's would be full, and she would have cookies for the kids. I always talk about Mammy as the 'baking cookies grandmother,' and I love that she called chocolate chip cookies 'chip chocolates,'" Janet adds.

1/2 teaspoon garlic salt

1/2 teaspoon salt

1 1/2 teaspoons chili powder, divided

1 boneless pork roast (4 to 5 pounds)

1 cup apple jelly

1 cup ketchup

2 tablespoons vinegar

1/2 cup crushed corn chips

---

1 Preheat the oven to 325 degrees.

2 In a small bowl combine the garlic salt, salt, and 1/2 teaspoon of the chili powder. Rub the mixture on all sides of the roast. Place the roast, fat side up, on a rack in a shallow roasting pan. Insert a meat thermometer into the thickest part of the roast, making sure the thermometer doesn't touch fat. Bake for 2 hours or until the thermometer reaches 165 degrees.

3 In a small saucepan combine the jelly, ketchup, vinegar, and remaining 1 teaspoon chili powder. Bring to a low boil, reduce the heat, and simmer for 2 minutes. Brush the roast with the jelly mixture. Sprinkle the crushed corn chips on top.

4 Return to the oven and bake for an additional 10 to 15 minutes or until the thermometer reaches 170 degrees. Serve sliced, warm, with sauce collected from the bottom of the pan.

MAKES 8 TO 10 SERVINGS.

KATHERINE A. FINCH (Forrest City, Arkansas) shares that in the years of the Depression, her grandmother, CLARA LILLIAN VERNON WADE (Fort Smith, Arkansas), used this recipe to feed many when her cupboard was all but bare. "No matter how hard the time, if you were seated at my grandmother's table, you were in clothes, with teeth and nails cleaned, hair combed, and socks on your feet. If not so attired, my grandfather would send you back to prepare yourself. He believed it was disrespectful to my grandmother to show up otherwise. It took only one time in pajamas for me to learn! While the Depression was over by the time I was born, we still enjoyed this meal and always had a crowd at the table," Katherine adds.

Cooking spray

2 medium onions, chopped

2 tablespoons butter

1 pound ground beef

1 teaspoon chili powder

1 (14.28 ounce) can tomato puree

1 cup water

2 cups pasta noodles, uncooked

Salt and black pepper to taste

1 (15 ounce) can whole kernel corn, drained

6 ripe olives, chopped

1 pimento, chopped

1 clove garlic, minced

1 cup grated cheese (any kind)

---

1 Preheat oven to 350 degrees. Lightly spray a 2-quart casserole dish.

2 In a large Dutch oven over medium-high heat, sauté the onions in butter. Add the ground beef and chili powder, and stir. Cook until the meat is browned. Add the tomato puree and water. Add the noodles and cook until tender. (More water may be added if needed.) Season to taste with salt and pepper. Add the corn, olives, pimento, and garlic and mix well.

3 Spoon into the casserole dish and top with the cheese. Bake approximately 45 minutes or until heated well through. Serve hot.

MAKES 6 SERVINGS.

CHICKEN AND DOOP

CORA ANNIE GALLIMORE was known to her grandchildren as Granny. She lived her entire life in Hinkledale, Tennessee. Granddaughter CINDY PREMO (Hermitage, Tennessee) shares that Granny showed her how a woman could be strong, self-sufficient, and do anything she wanted to do. Even though Granny had four children, a husband, and field hands to feed, there was always homemade fresh bread for three meals a day—made at that time using a wood stove. Back in the day, Cindy recalls not being fond of having to use an outhouse at Granny's; however, that small inconvenience paled in comparison to the many fond memories she and her sister have of summer days spent with Granny while their mom worked. Cindy shares, "Granny made incredible tea cakes, and one day she, my sister, and I were so engulfed in enjoying the first batch that none of us remembered there were still some in the oven until the kitchen was full of smoke. It's the only time we ever remember something she made not turning out perfectly. Instead of being angry, she dumped the burned ones—laughing with us the entire time—made a new tray, and baked them to perfection." Cindy says that Chicken and Doop is one of her favorite recipes from when she was a kid enjoying it at Granny's house or when her mom made it. A few years ago when Cindy lived in upstate New York, she cooked it to share her Southern heritage with her kids and family there. However, from their reaction, she's certain it must be an acquired Southern taste. (P.S. If you are asking what "doop" is, as we did, Cindy recalls Granny using "doop" to mean the cupboard is bare and you need to create a meal.)

---

1 whole chicken

1/8 teaspoon salt

1 (16 ounce) can chicken broth (optional)

1/4 cup white or brown vinegar*

Salt and black pepper to taste

1 1/2 teaspoons crushed red pepper flakes

1/4 cup self-rising flour

1/4 cup water

---

1 Cut the chicken into pieces and place in a large pot with enough water to cover. Add the salt and boil for approximately 45 minutes or until the meat is done. Remove the chicken and place it in a dish to cool. Save the broth from cooking the chicken and add canned broth if additional broth is desired. Add the vinegar, salt and pepper, and red pepper flakes to the broth.

2 In a separate cup or shaker, mix the flour and water well to make the thickener. Add the thickener to the broth gradually, stirring continuously.

3 When the chicken is cool, remove the fat and bones and pull the meat apart into small pieces. Discard the fat and bones and add the meat to the broth. Cook over low to medium heat until it reaches a slow boil. Continue cooking until the desired thickness is reached, approximately 15 minutes.

4 Taste for seasoning. Some folks add additional vinegar, crushed red pepper, salt, or pepper to their liking. Serve hot over homemade biscuits or waffles.

MAKES 8 SERVINGS.

* Do not use cider vinegar. "Brown" vinegar is malt vinegar.

MAMA KEE'S CHICKEN ROYALE

There's nothing better than a time-tested family recipe that gets passed down through the generations! And here's a great one from the McKee/Meadows/Strom line of cooks. Granddaughter KAY STROM (Bellevue, Tennessee) says this recipe of EDITH McKEE'S is a family favorite. Kay's mother got it from her mother, and she used to make it when Kay was growing up. Now Kay makes it for her husband and three children from time to time. Edith's three grandchildren called her Mama Kee. Mama Kee was born in Murfreesboro, Tennessee, and lived most of her life in Nashville, Tennessee.

Cooking spray

1 pound chicken, cooked and shredded

1 (8 ounce) package egg noodles cooked and drained

2 (14.25 ounce) cans cream of chicken soup

1 (4 ounce) can mushroom pieces, with juice

1 (16 ounce) container sour cream

1/4 teaspoon sage

1 Preheat the oven to 350 degrees. Lightly spray a 9 x 13-inch casserole dish.

2 In a large bowl combine the chicken, egg noodles, soup, mushroom pieces, sour cream, and sage. Mix well.

3 Spoon the mixture into the casserole dish and bake for 20 minutes or until heated well throughout. Serve hot.

MAKES 6 TO 8 SERVINGS.

VALLIE'S SUPPER-QUICK CASSEROLE

Grandson **GARY BROWN** (Bradyville, Tennessee) shares that his Grandma, **VALLIE MCGRAW**, currently lives in Beckley, West Virginia, which is the closest city to the little unincorporated town (Bolt) where she grew up before she married and ended up at Glen Rogers Mine. Gary says when they go to Grandma's house she will usually have her home-made yeast rolls ready or she'll make them at some point during their visit. Once when he heard West Virginia was expecting a huge snowstorm, he called her from Tennessee to make sure she was safe and to ask if she had stocked up on milk, bread, and other staples. "Grandma just chuckled and said if she needed bread, she would just make some! That put me in my modern-thinking place," Gary adds.

Cooking spray

1 1/2 pounds ground chuck

1 medium onion, chopped

1 (14.5 ounce) can mixed vegetables, drained

1 cup grated Cheddar cheese

1 (10.5 ounce) can cream of mushroom soup

1 (28 ounce) package tater tots

1 Preheat the oven to 350 degrees. Lightly spray a 9 x 13-inch casserole dish.
2 In a Dutch oven brown the meat and add the onion. When the meat is done cooking, drain off the grease. Add the mixed vegetables, cheese, and mushroom soup. Stir to combine.
3 Spoon the mixture into the casserole dish. Top with the tater tots and bake for 45 minutes.

MAKES 6 TO 8 SERVINGS.

To "keep God at the center of your marriage" is some great advice that Grandma BETTY KING (Candler, North Carolina) shared with her granddaughter, MEGAN KING HOOPINGARNER (Murfreesboro, Tennessee). Megan says, "My grandma met and married my grandpa nearly fifty-nine years ago. Since Grandpa was active duty in the army, they traveled together with their two children (my dad and my Aunt Cyndi) all over the U.S. and even overseas in Germany." Grandma says to this day that "Grandpa is the best thing that's ever happened to her!" Grandma also introduced Megan to real Southern cooking and baking and always makes everything from scratch.

I pound ground beef	1/2 cup water	6 hot dogs, cooked
I teaspoon salt	I teaspoon chili powder	6 hot dogs buns, split
I small onion, chopped	1/4 cup ketchup	

1 In a large skillet over medium-high heat, cook the ground beef, salt, and onion until the meat is browned. Drain off the grease.

2 Add the water and simmer for 20 minutes. Add the chili powder and ketchup and mix well. When heated well through, approximately 5 minutes, it's ready to serve. Spoon over warm hot dogs in buns.

MAKES 6 SERVINGS.

GRANDDADDY'S FAVORITE CASSEROLE

MEGAN KING HOOPINGARNER (Murfreesboro, Tennessee) shares that her Granny, BERNICE "CHRIS" HOWELL (Branford, Florida), met her granddaddy at a Halloween party thrown by his aunt. They were married in 1947 and moved shortly after into a house built by Megan's great-great-granddaddy in 1921. Megan recalls the Southern-style plantation home had a butler's pantry between the kitchen and dining room that stored a beautiful collection of Fiestaware. She adds, "While I didn't know the name at the time, I marveled at all of the different colors of the plates, bowls, and serving pieces that Granny had collected through the years, one piece at a time. I looked forward to finding out which color of plate I got at supper just as much as I did eating the hearty meals she created for us. To this day, the smell of cucumbers reminds me of her kitchen, as they were always on the counter, soaking in vinegar. Granny was able to get me to eat strawberries once I discovered they were irresistible when dipped in sugar. I also remember how odd it struck me as a kid of my generation, growing up mostly in suburbia, that my Granny could walk out her back door and eat blackberries right off the bush—I thought they came from the grocery store!"

Cooking spray

1 (16 ounce) box macaroni

1 teaspoon salt

1 (10.75 ounce) can cream of mushroom soup

Whole or 2 percent milk to fill half of soup can

2 cups sharp Cheddar cheese, shredded

1 (12 ounce) can Spam, cubed

1 (14 ounce) package herb seasoned stuffing mix, crushed

1 Preheat the oven to 350 degrees. Lightly spray a 2-quart casserole dish.

2 Cook the macaroni in salted water according to package directions. Drain when done and add to a large pan or bowl.

3 In a medium bowl mix the soup and milk and pour on the cooked macaroni. Add the cheese and Spam and mix well. Spoon into the casserole dish. Sprinkle the top with crushed stuffing before putting in the oven.

4 Bake for 30 minutes or until heated well through. Serve hot.

MAKES 6 SERVINGS.

Sitting in his grandmother's screened-in porch and looking out on the Chesapeake Bay in Virginia while enjoying a feast of corn, seafood, and sausage stew is a fond memory that comes to mind for **SCOTT YOUNG** (Franklin, Tennessee). Scott grew up in Richmond, Virginia, and shares that growing up, he spent a lot of time with his grandparents in the summertime. His grandmother was **GRACE WINGO** (Deltaville, Virginia). She was known as Nana to her four grandchildren. This stew is a family favorite, and while the "official" name for this dish is Frogmore Stew (named for the town near Beaufort, South Carolina, where it originated) the family thinks it's more fun to call it Froggy More Stew. Nana would cover a table with plastic, then newspaper, and give everyone a bowl for their shrimp shells before digging in!

2 pounds kielbasa or hot smoked sausage links*

1 1/2 gallons water (or enough to cover all ingredients)

1/4 cup Old Bay seasoning, plus extra for serving

4 pounds small red potatoes, whole

6 ears fresh corn, halved

4 pounds shrimp, unpeeled

Cocktail sauce

1 Cut the sausage into bite-size pieces.

2 Fill a large pot with water and Old Bay seasoning and bring to a rolling boil. Add the potatoes, return to a boil, and cook uncovered for 10 minutes.

3 Add the sausage pieces and corn halves and return to a boil. Cook until the potatoes are tender, approximately 15 minutes.

4 Add the shrimp to the pot and cook just 3 to 4 minutes or until the shrimp are pink. Be careful not to overcook the shrimp. Drain well and serve immediately with cocktail sauce and Old Bay seasoning to taste.

MAKES 8 TO 10 SERVINGS.

* Turkey kielbasa can also be used.

✕✕✕ SKILLET FRIED CHICKEN

While she has many fond memories of growing up on a farm, there are some things, like killing her own chickens, **SARAH SMITH** (Tupelo, Mississippi) is glad she no longer has to do! "We always had fresh chicken made with our own lard because we raised chicken and hogs. We had a large lard pail that I still remember—back then it was called a lard stand. And I still have the big black iron skillet and dome lid that my mother and grandmother, **SALLY LANGSTON** (Saltillo, Mississippi), used to use. Sometimes we'd even have fresh fried chicken for breakfast on Sunday mornings with homemade biscuits. If it was made for lunch or dinner, we'd enjoy the crispy fried chicken with turnip greens, butter beans, okra, or any other fresh vegetables from our garden," Sarah recalls.

I whole chicken	I 1/2 teaspoons salt	I 1/2 cups self-rising flour
2 large eggs	I teaspoon black pepper	
I cup whole milk or buttermilk		3 cups lard

1 Rinse the chicken thoroughly and cut into pieces. Place in a baking pan.

2 In a small bowl beat the eggs. Stir in the milk, salt, and pepper. Pour the milk mixture over the chicken pieces and allow to sit for 15 minutes.

3 Scoop the flour into a shallow dish with sides or into a plastic bag. Roll each piece of chicken in the flour, completely covering each piece. Set aside to dry.

4 Place the lard in a large cast-iron skillet and heat on medium to melt. When the fat reaches 350 degrees, it is ready. (Drop a pinch of flour in the hot grease to test. If it floats to the bottom, it's not hot enough. If it sizzles and floats on top, it's ready.)

5 Add chicken pieces to the skillet in a single layer and not touching each other. Reduce the heat to medium-low and fry the chicken slowly until golden brown, 12 to 14 minutes for larger pieces, or 7 to 8 minutes for smaller pieces, such as wings. Turn the chicken over and continue cooking until golden brown on the second side, 12 to 14 minutes for larger pieces, or 7 to 8 minutes for smaller pieces. (A meat thermometer should reach an internal temperature of 165 degrees, and juices should run clear.) When finished cooking, remove from the grease and drain on paper towels before serving.

MAKES 4 SERVINGS.

NOTE: *Cook the chicken in batches or use two skillets, if necessary. If cooking in batches, keep already cooked chicken warm in a very low oven (150–200 degrees), covered with foil.*

GRAMMY'S HOT CHICKEN SALAD CASSEROLE ✕✕✕

KENNAH MASON (Franklin, Tennessee) and her brothers have fond memories growing up in Texas and visiting their grandmother and great-grandmother in Lewisville, Texas, and climbing as high as they could on the big tree in their backyard. Their grandmother is LINDA TURMAN, a.k.a. Grammy, and their great-grandmother is BILLIE BUSHONG, a.k.a. Honey. Kennah shares, "When I would come into the house, they were always in the kitchen together, chatting away, but they would stop just long enough to say, 'There she is!' or 'Why, hello there, peanut,' or my favorite was when they called me 'little britches.' Once, during my junior year of college, Grammy and Honey drove all the way from Dallas, Texas, to watch me cheer at an Ohio State football game in Columbus, where I attended school. Honey was eighty-eight at the time, but she stuck it out and stayed the entire game!"

4 cups chopped chicken	1 tablespoon chopped onion	1 tablespoon lemon juice
4 large hard-boiled eggs, chopped	1 ½ cups mayonnaise	Cooking spray
2 cups diced celery	1 teaspoon salt	1 cup grated Cheddar cheese
1 cup sliced water chestnuts	1 teaspoon seasoned salt	1 ⅓ cups crushed potato chips

1 In a large bowl combine the chicken, eggs, celery, water chestnuts, onion, mayonnaise, salt, seasoned salt, and lemon juice.

2 Lightly spray a 9 x 13-inch baking pan. Spoon the chicken mixture into the prepared dish, cover, and refrigerate overnight.

3 When ready to bake, preheat the oven to 400 degrees. Sprinkle the cheese and crushed potato chips on top of the casserole. Bake for about 35 minutes or until bubbling hot.

MAKES 8 TO 10 SERVINGS.

Nana's Peanut Butter Pie

Summers Blackberry Cobbler

Grandmother Margaret's Apple Pie

Grandma Mac's Pecan Pie

Easy Layered Cobbler

Grandma's Chocolate Pie

Cherry-O Cream Pie

Granny's Rocky Road Pie

Crumb Top Apple Pie

Lemon Ice Box Pie

Make Ya Wanna Slap Your Grandma Chocolate Cobbler

Parthenia's Chess Pie

Page's Earth Grain Pie

Nama's Apple Dumplings

Erma's Easy Chess Pie

Nana Earlene's Chocolate Pie

Old-Fashioned Pumpkin Pie

Pies and Cobblers

NANA'S PEANUT BUTTER PIE

Granddaughter GENTRY ANNE HOLLIS (Nashville, Tennessee) got the beginning of her name from her grandmother's maiden name. SUSAN GENTRY WILLIAMS (also of Nashville) is known as Nana to Gentry Anne and her younger brother, Cal. This peanut butter pie is so easy to make that Gentry Anne and Cal only need a little help using the mixer. And for fun, they like to use a squeeze bottle filled with chocolate syrup to make faces on top of the pies.

I (8 ounce) package cream cheese, softened

I ½ cups powdered sugar

I cup peanut butter, extra crunchy

I (16 ounce) container frozen whipped topping, thawed

2 (9 inch) prepared chocolate cookie or chocolate graham cracker piecrusts

---

1 Using a hand mixer, beat together the cream cheese and powdered sugar. Mix in the peanut butter. Beat until smooth. Fold in the whipped topping. Spoon the mixture into two 9-inch piecrusts, cover, and freeze until firm.

MAKES 2 PIES; 16 SERVINGS.

SUMMERS BLACKBERRY COBBLER X X X

LUCY ADAMS REYNOLDS (Springfield, Tennessee) was known as Mammy to her grand-daughter, WANDA WATTS (also of Springfield). Mammy cooked on an old-fashioned wood stove when Wanda was a little girl, and on Sundays during the summer, she made blackberry cobbler in an oblong silver pan. She served cream in a small cat pitcher to pour on their cobbler. Wanda has that cat pitcher displayed in her kitchen today and says it brings a smile to her face each time she looks at it. Mammy also made small fried fruit pies during the winter months, using apples she dried during the summer on the tin roof that covered her well house.

1/3 cup lard or vegetable shortening, plus extra for preparing the pan

3/4 cup sugar

I tablespoon plus 2 cups all-purpose flour, divided

I 1/8 teaspoon salt, divided

3 cups washed and dried blackberries

3 teaspoons baking powder

2/3 cup whole milk

1/4 cup (1/2 stick) butter

1/2 teaspoon ground cinnamon

---

1 Preheat the oven to 425 degrees. Grease an 8-inch square baking pan.

2 In a medium bowl combine the sugar, I tablespoon of the flour, and 1/8 teaspoon of the salt. Add the berries and gently toss.

3 In a large bowl combine the remaining 2 cups flour, baking powder, the remaining I teaspoon salt, shortening, and milk. Divide the mixture in half. Roll out each portion of dough 1/4 inch thick. Fit the first rolled half of the dough into the baking pan.

4 Pour the fruit mixture into the pan, dot the fruit with butter and sprinkle with cinnamon. Use a biscuit cutter to cut 6 to 8 circles in the remaining dough and place on top of the fruit mixture.

5 Bake 30 minutes or until the fruit is bubbly and the biscuits are golden brown. If the biscuits on top are getting too brown before the fruit is bubbling, cover loosely with a piece of foil. Remove from the oven and place on a wire rack to cool slightly before serving. Serve alone or with whipped cream or vanilla ice cream. Refrigerate any leftovers and reheat before serving.

MAKES 6 TO 8 SERVINGS.

GRANDMOTHER MARGARET'S APPLE PIE ✕ ✕ ✕

MARGARET ROBINSON was born in Bluefield, West Virginia, and then lived in Woodlawn, Virginia. She was known as Grandmother Margaret to her grandchildren. Her grand-daughter, KATHRYN MITCHELL JOHNSON, born in Clemson, South Carolina, now calls Nashville, Tennessee, her home. Kathryn shares that her mother made her a book of their family's recipes. "That book is one of those things I would grab if there was an emergency and I only had time to pick up a few personal belongings," Kathryn says. "It is that spe-cial." One of the recipes in that special book is Grandmother Margaret's recipe for apple pie. It is a custard-type pie that Kathryn makes often, and it has become one of her family's favorites. However, she says that "it's kind of odd that we love it so much because it's the only good thing Grandmother Margaret ever cooked! She was known for her lime green Jell-O salads and her version of Hamburger Helper that we lovingly referred to (never to her face, of course) as 'Opossum Helper' because she cooked it so long the pasta began to break down. Anyway, this pie is good . . . I promise!"

I cup organic cane sugar

3 tablespoons all-purpose flour

1/2 cup unsalted butter, melted

2 large eggs, beaten

1/2 teaspoon ground cinnamon

1/2 teaspoon nutmeg

I teaspoon vanilla extract

3 cups apples,* peeled, cored, and chopped

I (9 inch) piecrust, unbaked

1 Preheat the oven to 425 degrees.

2 In a large bowl mix the sugar and flour together. Add the melted butter and eggs and stir to combine. Add the cinnamon, nutmeg, and vanilla, and then stir in the apples. Pour into the piecrust.

3 Bake for 15 minutes. Reduce the heat to 350 degrees and bake 30 to 35 minutes more until the apples are tender and the crust is golden brown.

MAKES 8 SERVINGS.

* Good baking apples include Granny Smith, Cortland, Rome, Northern Spy, Pink Lady, or a mix of any of them.

GRANDMA MAC'S PECAN PIE

ALIVIE ELIZABETH BRYAN MCPHERSON (Liberty, North Carolina) was known as Grandma Mac to her grandchildren. Granddaughter MARTHA DAVIS (Burlington, North Carolina) remembers having pecan trees on the farm where she was raised in Liberty, North Carolina. She shares that "Thanksgiving was the perfect time to make 'new crop' pecan pies. We would sit as a family to crack the pecans. After they were soaked in water, they were easier to crack, and we tried to get the 'meats' (pecans) out whole. There is still a pecan tree at the Bowman farm that was planted around 1905 when the farmhouse was built. It still produces pecans, and our brother owns the farm now." Today, Martha is a grandmother of five who loves to make this pie for her family during the holidays.

1/2 cup (1 stick) butter, softened

1/2 cup sugar

3 large eggs slightly beaten

3/4 cup dark corn syrup

1/4 teaspoon salt

1 teaspoon vanilla extract

1 cup chopped pecans

1 (9 inch) piecrust, unbaked, chilled but not frozen

---

1 Preheat the oven to 425 degrees.

2 Cream the butter, gradually adding the sugar and continuing to beat until light and fluffy. Add the eggs, corn syrup, salt, vanilla, and chopped nuts. Pour into the piecrust and place in the oven.

3 Bake for 10 minutes, reduce the heat to 325 degrees, and bake for an additional 35 minutes.

4 During the last 10 minutes of baking, cover the pie with foil or a foil pie pan to prevent the top of the pie from getting too hard. The pie is done when a knife inserted halfway between the center and the edge comes out clean. Cool the pie and serve plain. Or serve warm with ice cream or whipped cream.

MAKES 8 SERVINGS.

EASY LAYERED COBBLER ✕ ✕

ISABELLE HUDSON IKARD PEARSALL was born in Sparta, Tennessee, and has lived in Nashville, Tennessee, since she married Sam "Sparky" Pearsall in 1946. They are parents to four children, grandparents to seven, and great-grandparents to five. Isabelle remembers spending summers with her grandmother, ISABELLE HUDSON (Sparta, Tennessee), where she learned to quilt and sew. Isabelle admits to many mishaps in the kitchen in the early days of her marriage to Sam, including burning baked potatoes and pork chops and accidentally putting lemon oil on the table to eat with cooked turnip greens, instead of vinegar! However, her aunt gave her the *Joy of Cooking* (which she still has today), and Isabelle claims it was a lifesaver! She's proud to say she and Sam learned to cook, and they raised four healthy children. And she went on to teach all of them to cook.

Vegetable shortening for preparing pan

1 (30 ounce) can apple or cherry pie filling

1 (8 ounce) can crushed pineapple, undrained

1 (9 ounce) box golden yellow cake mix

1/2 cup (1 stick) butter, melted

---

1 Preheat the oven to 425 degrees. Grease an 8 x 8-inch baking pan.
2 Spread the pie filling and pineapple on the bottom of the baking pan. Sprinkle the dry cake mix on top of the fruit mixture. Drizzle melted butter over the top of the cake mix. Bake for 25 to 30 minutes or until golden brown. Serve warm. Refrigerate any leftovers.

MAKES 6 TO 8 SERVINGS.

GRANDMA'S CHOCOLATE PIE

Grandchildren **NATHANIEL** and **KAYLEE STINSON** (Scottsville, Kentucky) share that it always smells so good in Grandma's kitchen because she's usually in there cooking something wonderful! Their grandma, **DEBBIE MCMURTRY** (Westmoreland, Tennessee), has been known to say, "Nothing says loving like something from the oven" and "God gave you two good hands, so use them as your tools for baking or cooking something wonderful in the kitchen." At Easter she always makes resurrection rolls. They are yummy, and as she makes them, she shares the story of Jesus and how he died for us on the cross and arose again on the third day. Regarding this particular pie, Grandma's says, "It's real good hot, wonderful cold, and you can even eat it frozen—then it's like a Popsicle!"

PIE:

1 (9-inch) piecrust, unbaked

3/4 cups sugar

5 tablespoons all-purpose flour

1/4 teaspoon salt

4 tablespoons cocoa or 1 1/2 squares baking chocolate

2 large egg yolks, beaten slightly (save the whites for meringue)

1 1/2 cups whole milk

1/2 teaspoon vanilla extract

1 tablespoon butter

MERINGUE:

2 large egg whites

1/8 teaspoon salt

4 tablespoons sugar

1 Preheat the oven to 350 degrees.
2 **TO MAKE THE PIE**, poke holes in the unbaked piecrust with a fork. Bake it until it is lightly brown, about 20 minutes. Remove from the oven.
3 While the piecrust is baking, in a medium saucepan combine the sugar, flour, salt, cocoa, egg yolks, and milk with a whisk. While stirring, cook over medium heat until it bubbles and thickens, 5 to 10 minutes. If it becomes lumpy, beat out the lumps with the whisk.
4 Remove from the heat and stir in the vanilla and butter. Allow to cool for 25 to 30 minutes and then pour into the baked piecrust.

5 To MAKE THE MERINGUE, beat the egg whites with salt, and when they start to get fluffy, add the sugar. The meringue is done when it is stiff and peaks. Top the pie with the meringue mixture. Bake until the peaks on the meringue are lightly browned, about 10 minutes. Serve warm.

MAKES 8 SERVINGS.

CHERRY-O CREAM PIE

"We all go to the beach for one week in the summer and again at Thanksgiving and stay in Nini and Papa's condo in Destin, Florida. My mom says we've been going there ever since we were babies. My younger brothers and I really enjoy that special time with our grandparents," shares granddaughter MADDIE STROM (Bellevue, Tennessee). Her Nini, SANDRA MEADOWS (Nashville, Tennessee), was born in Murfreesboro, Tennessee, and is a grandmother of four. Maddie says this is one of her absolute favorite things that Nini makes!

---

1 (8 ounce) package cream cheese, softened

1 (15 ounce) can sweetened condensed milk

1/3 cup lemon juice

1 teaspoon vanilla extract

1 (9-inch) graham cracker piecrust

1 (30 ounce) can cherry pie filling

---

1 In a large bowl use a hand mixer to beat the cream cheese until smooth. Add the milk and mix well. Add the lemon juice and vanilla and mix well. Pour the mixture into the piecrust and chill for 2 to 3 hours in the refrigerator. Top with the cherry pie filling right before eating.

MAKES 8 SERVINGS.

GRANNY'S ROCKY ROAD PIE ✕ ✕ ✕

CLINT McCULLOCH (Lebanon, Tennessee) says he could eat this whole pie by himself! He remembers that once in her later years, his Granny, ANNE DUGAN (Nashville, Tennessee), accidently put dried beans in this pie instead of chocolate chips. "Boy, was that first bite a surprise. We now refer to this as 'Granny's Bean Pie,'" he says. As a toddler, Clint and his two brothers would often spend the weekend with their grandparents while their mother worked as a nurse. Granny worked, too, and on Friday afternoon when she got off work, their mother would meet her in Nashville, and Granny would take the boys home with her for the weekend. While his brothers rode in the backseat, Clint stood up next to Granny in the front seat (long before child restraint laws, of course). "Granny and Granddaddy always took us to eat fast food while we were there. But her cooking was better! Granny was a hard worker. She loved me and my brothers dearly and gave up a lot of weekends for us," he adds.

2 (9 inch) graham cracker piecrusts

1 (1.5 ounce) box instant chocolate pudding mix

1 cup whole milk

1 (16 ounce) large container whipped topping

1 cup miniature marshmallows

3/4 cup semisweet chocolate chips

1 Preheat the oven to 350 degrees.
2 Bake the piecrusts for 10 minutes; then remove from the oven and cool.
3 In a large bowl stir the pudding mix and milk. Add the whipped topping and mix well. Fold in the marshmallows and chocolate chips. Divide the filling between the 2 piecrusts. Refrigerate 2 hours or until you just can't stand it anymore and have to have a piece. Keep refrigerated.

MAKES 2 PIES; 8 SERVINGS EACH.

CRUMB TOP APPLE PIE

While some grandmothers are cake makers and some are pie makers, granddaughters **ADDISON ELIZABETH SMITH** (Johnson City, Tennessee), **ISABEL KATHLEEN SHEFFIELD** (Nashville, Tennessee), and **REESE ELIZABETH SHEFFIELD** (also of Nashville) say that their Grandmama is definitely a pie lady! They share that **ELIZABETH ROBERTSON SMITH** (Rogersville, Tennessee) makes this pie for every occasion—birthdays, holidays, family gatherings—and that everyone loves it! The girls love her famous pie too—especially when eaten warm with ice cream. While still little girls now, they look forward to Grandmama teaching them how to make it so they'll be sure the tradition lives on!

APPLE BASE:

Butter to grease dish

6 cups apples, peeled, cored, and sliced (approximately 6 medium)*

1/2 cup sugar

2 tablespoons all-purpose flour

1 teaspoon ground cinnamon

1/2 teaspoon salt

TOPPING:

1 cup all-purpose flour

1/2 cup firmly packed brown sugar

1/2 cup (1 stick) cold margarine

1 Preheat the oven to 350 degrees. Butter the bottom and sides of a 9 x 11-inch baking pan.

2 **TO MAKE THE BASE**, place the apples in a large bowl and add the sugar, flour, cinnamon, and salt. Toss to coat the apples and spread out evenly in the buttered baking pan.

3 **TO MAKE THE TOPPING**, in a medium bowl use a pastry blender to combine the flour, brown sugar, and margarine until crumbly. Spread the topping over the apples and bake 35 to 40 minutes or until the apples are tender and the mixture is brown and bubbly. Serve warm, alone or with vanilla ice cream.

MAKES 8 TO 10 SERVINGS.

* Good baking apples include Granny Smith, Cortland, Rome, Northern Spy, Pink Lady, or a mix of any of them.

LEMON ICE BOX PIE ✕ ✕ ✕

LUCY HARRIS (Weir, Mississippi) was known as Mamaw Lucy to great-granddaughter, **LARISSA ARNAULT** (Nashville, Tennessee). Until she was five years old, Larissa lived just down the hill from her Mamaw Lucy and Papaw Orn. A large garden separated their houses, and she remembers helping Mamaw Lucy pick butter beans and purple hull peas from those rows. The family all lived on a big hill—she and her parents at the bottom of the hill, Mamaw and Papaw Harris in the middle, and her grandparents (Mamaw Sarah and Papaw Frankie Arnault) at the top.

1 (12 ounce) box vanilla wafers

1/4 cup (1/2 stick) butter, melted

3 large eggs, room temperature and separated

1 (14.5 ounce) can sweetened condensed milk

1/3 cup lemon juice

1/4 teaspoon cream of tartar

6 tablespoons sugar

1 Preheat broiler to 500 degrees.

2 Crush enough of the vanilla wafers to make 1 1/2 cups. Mix with the butter. Press crust into a 9-inch pie pan.

3 Beat together the egg yolks and sweetened condensed milk. Slowly beat in the lemon juice. Beat until very thick. Pour the mixture into the piecrust.

4 In a glass bowl use a hand mixer to beat together the egg whites and cream of tartar. Add the sugar 1 tablespoon at a time, beating after each addition. Beat on high until stiff peaks form. Layer evenly on top of the lemon pie.

5 Place in the oven and brown just until the meringue is set and golden. Watch closely so the meringue does not burn.

6 Line the edges of the crust with whole vanilla wafers to garnish. Cool before serving. Keep the pie refrigerated.

MAKES 8 SERVINGS.

MAKE YA WANNA SLAP YOUR GRANDMA ✕ ✕ ✕
CHOCOLATE COBBLER

Grandchildren DUSTIN and JENNY MCMURTRY (Scottsville, Kentucky) share that their Nashville, Tennessee–born and Hendersonville, Tennessee–raised Grandma, DEBBIE MCMURTRY, now lives in Westmoreland, Tennessee. They say that "Grandma always makes things fun whether we are cooking together in the kitchen or just sitting around her table to eat. We always learn something from her, and she always encourages us to try new things and to try and enjoy whatever life brings."

---

6 tablespoons butter

I cup self-rising flour

I 3/4 cups sugar, divided

1/4 cup plus I 1/2 tablespoons unsweetened cocoa, divided

1/2 cup whole milk

I teaspoon vanilla extract

I 1/2 cups boiling water

---

1 Preheat the oven to 350 degrees. Place the butter in an 8 x 8-inch baking pan and melt while the oven preheats.

2 In a medium bowl stir together the flour, 3/4 cup of the sugar, and I 1/2 tablespoons of the cocoa. Stir in the milk and vanilla until smooth. Spoon this batter over the melted butter in the baking pan.

3 Stir together the remaining I cup of sugar and 1/4 cup cocoa. Sprinkle over the batter. Slowly pour boiling water over the top of the mixture. Bake for 30 minutes until set. Serve slightly warm, alone or with vanilla ice cream.

MAKES 9 TO 12 SERVINGS.

PARTHENIA'S CHESS PIE

MELANIE MARTIN (Nashville, Tennessee) is originally from Crossville, Alabama. Her grandmother was PARTHENIA SHEARON BOYCE, who lived most of her adult life in Wartrace, Tennessee. Melanie shares, "Parthenia was a widow, and she remarried two weeks before I was born. She moved from her home in Wartrace, Tennessee, to Shelbyville, Tennessee, to begin married life again. We made the two-and-a-half-hour drive to Shelbyville about every other month, always arriving at lunchtime on Saturday. And what a lunch we would arrive to! While I know this can't be true, it seemed like every time she cooked we had vegetables, good ol' country ham, and biscuits. I could (and sometimes tried to) make an entire meal out of her biscuits, which she made by the recipe on the White Lily flour bag. And of course, there was always dessert." Melanie adds that this chess pie is guaranteed to be an authentic Southern-style favorite and not a Yankee imitation.

1/2 cup (1 stick) butter

1 1/2 cups sugar

3 large eggs, slightly beaten

1 1/2 teaspoons vinegar

1 1/2 teaspoons cornmeal

2 tablespoons buttermilk

1 teaspoon vanilla extract

1 (9 inch) piecrust, unbaked

---

1 Preheat the oven to 425 degrees.
2 Melt the butter in a saucepan over medium heat. Stir in the sugar. Remove from the heat. Add the eggs, vinegar, cornmeal, buttermilk, and vanilla and blend well. Pour into the piecrust.
3 Bake for 10 minutes, reduce the heat to 350 degrees, and bake until the filling shakes slightly and is brown, about 20 minutes.

MAKES 8 SERVINGS.

PAGE'S EARTH GRAIN PIE ✕ ✕ ✕

DAVID PAGE (Franklin, Tennessee) was born in Nashville, Tennessee. His grandmother is MAXINE PAGE (also of Nashville), who is affectionately known to her grandchildren as Page. David says, "I don't know how she does it, but Page always has delicious food ready and waiting at her house. Everyone's favorite is this earth grain pie, and we all fight over who gets a piece. When I was little, we always ate at Page's house after church on Sunday. She wouldn't just have one meat and three vegetables . . . she would have two or three meats and about six vegetables. Dessert was always a treat because everyone had their personal favorite, and she had usually made them all. Page loves for us to eat. While she takes great joy in preparing meals for our family, there's even greater joy in watching all of us eat until we are full!"

½ cup (1 stick) margarine

4 large eggs

1 cup corn syrup

1 (12 ounce) package semisweet chocolate chips

1 cup pecans, whole and pieces

1 cup sugar

1 cup shredded coconut

2 (9 inch) piecrusts, unbaked

---

1 Preheat the oven to 350 degrees.

2 In a saucepan over medium heat, melt the margarine and add the eggs and corn syrup. Blend well. Gently add the chocolate chips, pecans, sugar, and coconut, and mix well. Pour into the 2 piecrusts.

3 Bake for 40 minutes or until set. If the edges are starting to brown too much, wrap them with foil for the remainder of the baking time. Serve warm or at room temperature.

MAKES 2 PIES; 8 SERVINGS EACH.

NAMA'S APPLE DUMPLINGS

CHARLOTTE FERKAN PORTER is known as Nama to youngest granddaughters AVA and LILLIAN PORTER and as Grandma to oldest granddaughters SOPHIA and OLIVIA PORTER. While Charlotte isn't from the South, author Faye Porter shares that because Charlotte is her mum, and a grandma, and a great baker, and has kids that live in the South, we wanted to include her! And we had to include Charlotte's apple dumplings because Faye says these are her absolute favorite thing her mum bakes. Whether coming home from college or coming from Nashville to visit her parents now, Faye shares that "when my mum asks, 'What are you hungry for that you'd like me to make?' hands down the reply is these apple dumplings!" Faye's dad and three brothers are also fans of these delicious gems. And while they're great served warm with vanilla bean ice cream, Faye loves them cold the next day when the bottom dough is even softer.

6 small to medium apples[*]

SYRUP:

1 1/2 cups sugar

2 cups water

1/2 teaspoon ground cinnamon

1/2 cup (1 stick) butter

DOUGH:

2 cups all-purpose flour, plus extra for rolling dough

3/4 cup vegetable shortening

1 teaspoon salt

2 teaspoons baking powder

1/2 cup whole milk

INSIDE APPLES:

Cinnamon to sprinkle

3 teaspoons butter, divided

1 Peel and core the apples. Leave whole or quarter them.

2 TO MAKE THE SYRUP, in a saucepan combine the sugar, water, and cinnamon and cook over medium heat until the mixture reaches a low boil. Remove from the heat and add the butter. Set aside to cool for approximately 20 minutes.

3 TO MAKE THE DOUGH, preheat the oven to 375 degrees.

4 In a large bowl combine the flour, shortening, salt, baking powder, and milk and mix well by hand as you would for a piecrust. Divide the dough into 6 balls of equal size. Roll out one portion at a time on a lightly floured surface.

5 In the center of each dough "circle," place a whole apple or four apple quarters standing upright. Inside the whole apple or on top of the quartered apples, sprinkle the cinnamon and add 1/2 teaspoon of the butter. Bring the dough up over the sides of each apple and press together at the top.

6 Place 3 dumplings each into 2 large ungreased loaf pans (9.75 x 5.75 x 2.75-inch size each). It's important that the sides of your pan be 2 inches or higher to prevent hot syrup from running over during baking.

7 Pour half of the syrup over the three dumplings in one pan and the remaining half over the dumplings in the other pan. Bake for 35 to 40 minutes or until nicely browned on top.

8 During the last 20 minutes, use a spoon to collect the syrup at the bottom of the pan and baste the dumplings three times. Serve warm or cold. (It's doubtful, but if there happen to be any leftovers, refrigerate.)

MAKES 6 DUMPLINGS.

* Good baking apples include Granny Smith, Cortland, Rome, Northern Spy, Pink Lady, or a mix of any of them.

✗✗✗ ERMA'S EASY CHESS PIE

CHIP McGEE (Nashville, Tennessee) was born in Corinth, Mississippi, because that was the location of the hospital closest to Acton, Tennessee, where his parents lived. But that gave him a connection to each of his parents' home states since his mom was from Mississippi and his dad from Tennessee. Chip remembers his grandmother, ERMA SMITH (Tupelo, Mississippi), as a small and quiet woman who liked to stay "in the know" with the latest and greatest news about town. His earliest memories of his grandmother were of her with very long, white hair, down to the back of her knees. He remembers his Aunt Sarah combing Grandmother's hair, creating a long braid, and then fixing it into a bun. In her later years, he remembers when she cut the long hair off into a short style that required weekly visits to a local beauty shop. Chip loved spending summers and Christmases at Granddad and Grandmother's—Grandmother was an incredible cook. Chip's all-time favorites would have to be her chicken and dumplins, biscuits with chocolate gravy, and this chess pie.

I cup sugar

1/2 cup (I stick) margarine, softened

3 large egg yolks

1/4 cup all-purpose flour

1/4 cup whole milk

I teaspoon vanilla extract

I (9 inch) piecrust, unbaked

---

1 Preheat the oven to 350 degrees.

2 In a medium bowl mix the sugar, margarine, egg yolks, flour, milk, and vanilla together. Pour into the unbaked piecrust and bake for approximately 45 minutes or until the center is set and a toothpick stuck in the middle of the pie comes out clean.

MAKES 8 SERVINGS.

NANA EARLENE'S CHOCOLATE PIE ✕ ✕ ✕

"Second to a relationship with God, a good education is the most important thing you can have," and "Always be kind to others and take care of your family when they are in need" are what **CHUCK HARRIS** (Murfreesboro, Tennessee) says he's learned from his Nana, **EARLENE GOARD** (also of Murfreesboro). Chuck shares that "Nana would take me to Gatlinburg, Tennessee, every year to spend time in the Great Smoky Mountains. She absolutely loved Dolly Parton, so we would always visit Dollywood." One of Nana's favorite sayings is, "You would argue with the devil!" Nana also makes the best breakfasts Chuck has ever eaten, always cooking so much food! This pie is one of his personal favorites.

FILLING:

3 large egg yolks

3 tablespoons all-
   purpose flour

1 cup sugar

2 cups 2 percent milk

3 tablespoons cocoa

1 (9 inch) piecrust,
   baked

MERINGUE:

3 large egg whites

1 tablespoon sugar

1/2 tablespoon vanilla
   extract

1 TO MAKE THE FILLING, in a medium saucepan combine the egg yolks, flour, sugar, milk, and cocoa. Stir over medium heat until the pie filling thickens, 8 to 10 minutes. Pour the pie filling into the piecrust and let it sit until cool, about 30 minutes.

2 Preheat the oven to 425 degrees.

3 TO MAKE THE MERINGUE, beat the egg whites on high with a mixer until stiff peaks form. Gradually add the sugar and vanilla and continuing beating until the meringue is fluffy. Spoon the meringue on top of the pie and spread to the edges to seal the crust.

4 Bake for just 3 to 5 minutes until the tips of the meringue are browned. Cool on a wire rack before slicing.

MAKES 8 SERVINGS.

OLD-FASHIONED PUMPKIN PIE ✕ ✕ ✕

"See here" was how grandmother CAROLINE BENEDICT (Nashville, Tennessee) would often preface an important statement. Caroline was the mother to four and grandmother to sixteen! She was in her seventies by the time her youngest grandchild, CLARA MAY BENEDICT (also of Nashville), came along. Clara May shares that as her grandmother aged, she was less active, with one of her older daughters doing the cooking. So Clara May actually learned most about her paternal grandmother's cooking and baking from her own mother, who was very close to her mother-in-law and passed down Caroline's recipes, many of which were from the late 1800s. This moist and delicious pumpkin pie was a Benedict family favorite at the holidays. Clara has adapted her grandmother's recipe for the convenience of canned pumpkin and store-bought crusts.

1 teaspoon all-purpose flour	1/2 teaspoon allspice	1 cup whole milk
2 cups sugar	3 large eggs	2 (9 inch) piecrusts, unbaked
Pinch of salt	1/4 cup (1/2 stick) butter, melted	
1 teaspoon ground cinnamon	1 (15 ounce) can pure pumpkin	

1 Preheat the oven to 350 degrees.
2 In a large bowl mix the flour into the sugar. Add the salt, cinnamon, and allspice. In a small bowl beat the eggs and then add to the flour mixture.
3 Stir in the melted butter, pumpkin, and then the milk. Mix well and pour into two unbaked piecrusts.
4 Bake for 50 minutes, or until the center is no longer liquid. Be careful not to overbake. Cool completely on wire racks until serving or before refrigerating.

MAKES 2 PIES; 16 SERVINGS.

Iced Fudge Layer Cake

North Carolina Pound Cake

Grandma Burkett's Syrup Cake

Chocolate Lava Cake

Grana's Plum Cake

Mom Mom's Almond Torte

Nanny's Coconut Cracker Cake

Buttermilk Iced Plum Cake

Christmas Cake à la Mary

Lorraine's Double Chocolate
   Cake

Granny's Skillet Pineapple
   Upside-Down Cake

No-Bake Refrigerator Cake

Nama's Texas Sheet Cake

Nanny Patsy's Favorite Chocolate
   Shortcake

Sandra's Strawberry Cake

Lizzie's Angel Food Cake

Grandmama's Pound Cake

Granny's Blackberry Cake

Chocolate Éclair Cake

Grandmother's Lemon Cheese Cake

Lemon Supreme Pound Cake

Nonna's Iced Banana Cake

Grandmother's Pound Cake

Mom's 5-Flavor Cake

Nanny's Coconut Cake

Cakes

DONNA DELEON now lives in Aurora, Colorado, but she was born and raised in Arkansas. Donna shares that her Grandma, ETHEL FREE (Vilonia, Arkansas), told her a story about something that happened between her grandparents when they were newlyweds. Back then you starched clothes by mixing your own starch solution with water and putting it in a bottle to shake onto the clothes as you were ironing them (with your iron that was heated on the wood stove). You adjusted the "stiffness" of the starching by putting more or less water into the starch. Grandpa complained that she had not starched his shirts stiff enough to suit him. Irritated, Grandma took a pair of his boxer shorts and starched them so stiff that when dried, they stood up by themselves! She then left them on Grandpa's bedside table for him to find the next morning. While Donna still doesn't know who won the argument over "how much starch is enough," she's never been able to get the thought of those super-stiff, standing boxer shorts out of her mind. Donna shares that her Grandma made this iced fudge layer cake for every family get-together.

CAKE:

Butter and flour to prepare pan

4 ounces unsweetened chocolate

6 tablespoons water

1 1/2 cups sugar, divided

1/2 cup vegetable shortening

1 teaspoon vanilla extract

3 large eggs

2 cups cake flour

1 teaspoon baking soda

1/4 teaspoon salt

2/3 cup whole milk

ICING:

2 ounces unsweetened chocolate, in bits

4 tablespoons butter

1 1/2 cups sugar

1 tablespoon corn syrup

1/2 cup whole milk

1/4 teaspoon salt

1 teaspoon vanilla extract

1 Preheat the oven to 350 degrees. Grease and lightly flour two 9-inch cake pans. (Grandma would actually use powdered sugar as the dusting powder.)

(CONTINUED ON NEXT PAGE)

2 **To make the cake,** put the chocolate, water, and $1/2$ cup of the sugar in a heavy-bottomed pan over low heat, stirring often. As the chocolate melts, stir vigorously to blend. Cook until the chocolate has completely melted and the mixture is smooth.

3 Cream the shortening and remaining sugar together until light. Add the vanilla and beat until well blended. Add the eggs, one at a time, beating thoroughly after each addition.

4 Sift the flour, baking soda, and salt together on a piece of wax paper. Add the flour mixture alternately with the milk in three parts to the shortening mixture. Add the chocolate mixture and beat until well blended. Pour the batter into the pans.

5 Bake for 35 to 40 minutes, or until a straw inserted in the center comes out dry. Cool in the pans for 10 minutes; then turn the cakes out on racks to cool. Cool cakes completely before icing.

6 **To make the icing,** stir together the chocolate, butter, sugar, corn syrup, milk, and salt in a heavy-bottomed pan. Bring to a rolling boil and cook, stirring vigorously, for just one minute; cool. Add the vanilla and beat until thick. Ice the middle, top, and sides of a 9-inch two-layer cake (if you don't eat too much while "testing" it).

MAKES 10 TO 12 SERVINGS.

NORTH CAROLINA POUND CAKE ✕ ✕ ✕

LINDA LEDFORD PORTER now lives in Swartz Creek, Michigan, but she was born and raised in Spruce Pine, North Carolina. Her grandma, FLORENCE DELLINGER MCKINNEY (also of Spruce Pine), was one of eight children and lived to be ninety-two years old. Linda remembers that Grandma loved sweet stuff, making it for her family and for "decoration days"—days at church, when they decorated graves at the church and had a huge potluck meal. Grandma knew all the old health remedies from the Depression days, and one of her favorites was the use of sassafras tea, said to help with bronchitis, gout, and arthritis. Linda's family once took her for a ride on the Blue Ridge Parkway, and Grandma said, "It seems like I've been around the world." One of Grandma's funny sayings was, "That person is meaner than a striped snake; bless their heart, they better get right with the Lord." She also shares that her grandma, whom she loved so very much, taught her to can, bake, cook, and pray.

I cup (2 sticks) butter, softened, plus extra to prepare pan

1/2 cup vegetable shortening

3 cups sugar

I cup whole milk

5 large eggs

3 1/2 cups all-purpose flour

I teaspoon salt

I tablespoon lemon juice

I teaspoon vanilla extract

Powdered sugar (optional)

Fresh berries (optional)

Whipped topping (optional)

---

1 Preheat the oven to 350 degrees. Grease a tube pan.
2 In a large bowl use a hand mixer to cream together the butter, shortening, and sugar. Add the milk and blend. Add one egg at a time, alternating with about I cup of flour at a time and beating after each addition.
3 Add the salt, lemon juice, and vanilla and blend. Pour the batter into the tube pan and bake for I hour and I5 minutes.
4 Serve with powdered sugar, fresh berries, or whipped topping. As Grandma used to say: "Cut in slivers it serves a lot; cut in big chunks and it might not."

MAKES 8 SERVINGS.

GRANDMA BURKETT'S SYRUP CAKE

When they were young girls, sisters JULIE THREET (Burns, Tennessee), SHELLEY GREER (Fairview, Tennessee), and BRENDA OLIPHANT (also of Fairview) share that they would travel to Grandma Burkett's "house on the hill" for special holidays to gather with family from several states. "Grandma, SARAH BEATRICE BURKETT (born in Anderson, South Carolina), always cooked a grand meal, occasionally stopping to dab her perspiration with the hanky she kept tucked in her cleavage. We used to ask if she was crying and she'd say, 'No, honey, just perspiring. Not sweating, because ladies don't sweat.' We all sat down at the large dining table (some had to sit at the small table in the kitchen) to devour the meal, and then afterward came the music—rhythm guitars, glorious voices, and lots of laughter. With a little encouragement, Grandma would sit down at the upright piano and play some old tunes by ear. And last but not least would come Grandma's syrup cake! She took such care to make the cake just right, and it was usually accompanied with rich coffee made from the percolator on the stove. Oftentimes the cake leaned a little (despite the box of toothpicks) from the weight of the syrupy icing drizzled throughout and on top. But there was never one crumb left. Grandma showered us all with her love through the carefully prepared meals, her musical influence, and THE cake."

CAKE:

2/3 cup vegetable shortening, melted, plus extra for preparing pans

2 1/2 cups sifted cake flour, plus more

for flouring the pans

1 teaspoon salt

1 2/3 cups sugar

3 1/3 teaspoons baking powder

3/4 cup whole milk

3 large eggs, unbeaten

1 1/2 teaspoons vanilla extract

SYRUP:

1/2 cup whole milk

3 (3 ounce) squares unsweetened chocolate, cut up

1 teaspoon light corn syrup

Dash of salt

1 1/2 cups sugar

2 teaspoons butter

1 teaspoon vanilla extract

1 Preheat the oven to 350 degrees. Lightly coat 2 (9-inch) cake pans with shortening. Lightly flour both pans and shake out excess flour.

2 TO MAKE THE CAKE, in a large bowl use a hand mixer to combine the shortening, cake flour, salt, sugar, baking powder, and milk thoroughly for 2 minutes at medium speed. Then add the eggs and vanilla and mix thoroughly another 2 minutes.

3 Pour the batter into the prepared pans and bake approximately 30 minutes until a toothpick inserted into the middle comes out clean. Cool cakes in the pans on wire racks for 20 minutes. Remove the cakes from the pans and return to the wire racks until completely cool.

4 TO MAKE THE SYRUP, combine the milk, chocolate, corn syrup, salt, sugar, and butter in a saucepan. Stir over low heat until the chocolate melts. Bring to a soft rolling boil, stirring constantly. Boil 1 minute. Remove from the heat, add the vanilla, and stir, stir, stir. Continue stirring until smooth and drizzly.

5 To assemble the cake, slice both cakes into horizontal layers and brush away any excess crumbs. Place one split layer on a plate. Drizzle 1/4 of the syrup over the layer. Top with the next layer and drizzle another 1/4 of the syrup over the top. Repeat with the third cake layer and 1/4 syrup and top with the final cake layer. Drizzle remaining syrup over the top of cake. You may need to secure the layers with toothpicks.

MAKES 8 TO 10 SERVINGS.

LILI HARRIS (Murfreesboro, Tennessee) enjoys playing baby dolls, coloring, watching movies, and swimming with her grandma, KATHY WILLIAMS. Kathy was born in Clarksville, Tennessee, and now lives in Murfreesboro. Lili shares that Grandma likes to bake yummy things and spend lots of time in her garden. "My grandma wanted my dad to have a good vocabulary, so she read books to him every night. My dad and I read books every night too," Lili adds.

CAKE:

Vegetable shortening to prepare custard cups	6 ounces semisweet baking chocolate	3 large eggs
	6 ounces butter, softened, diced	$1/2$ cup sugar
		3 cups all-purpose flour

VANILLA CREAM SAUCE:

I cup whipping cream	$1/2$ vanilla bean, split lengthwise	3 egg yolks
2 tablespoons sugar		

RASPBERRY GARNISH:

10 to 12 large raspberries, fresh or frozen	I teaspoon sugar, more to taste	I teaspoon cornstarch

1 Preheat the oven to 350 degrees. Lightly grease 4 individual custard cups or ramekins and place on a cookie sheet.

2 TO MAKE THE CAKE, in a double boiler on low heat, melt the chocolate, stirring constantly. When melted, remove from the heat. Stir in the diced butter until it melts.

3 In a large bowl beat together the eggs and sugar. Stir in the melted chocolate and then the flour.

4 Pour the chocolate batter into the greased custard cups. Bake for approximately 12 minutes, until the edges are set. The middle should remain soft.

5 Remove from the oven and let cool for 5 minutes. Loosen the edges of the cakes with a knife and transfer to 4 separate dessert plates while still warm.

(CONTINUED ON NEXT PAGE)

6 **TO MAKE THE VANILLA CREAM SAUCE,** in a medium saucepan over medium-low heat, combine the cream and sugar. Scrape the vanilla bean seeds into the pan. Add the pod. Bring the mixture just to a boil (do not let it boil or it may curdle).

7 In a medium bowl whisk the egg yolks. Whisk half of the cream and sugar mixture into the egg yolks. Return the mixture to the saucepan and cook until thickened, stirring constantly, about 5 minutes. Strain into a bowl. Cover and refrigerate until ready to use. This can be made ahead of time.

8 **TO MAKE THE RASPBERRY GARNISH,** put fresh or frozen raspberries in a food processor for a few seconds, add sugar to taste; then strain.

9 In a small saucepan, heat the strained raspberry mixture and add the cornstarch, stirring to mix well. Remove from the heat, transfer to a small bowl, cover, and refrigerate until ready to use. This can be made ahead of time.

10 To serve, spoon the vanilla sauce around each chocolate lava cake on a dessert plate, and dot with the raspberry garnish.

MAKES 4 SERVINGS.

GRANA'S PLUM CAKE

DIVYA FAITH KARCHER (Nashville, Tennessee) is the second of two granddaughters for CHRISTINE KARCHER (also of Nashville). Christine was born in England and raised in Shreveport, Louisiana. She is affectionately known as Mimi or Grana to the girls. While Divya is still a little one, she enjoys splashing in the pool and playing games with Grana and big sister, Zivah. While Grana says the little girls are still developing their tastes, she sure hopes they will enjoy Louisiana and Southern cooking and learning about family traditions as they grow up.

2 (1 pound, 12 ounce) cans red plums or 14 fresh dark purple plums

3 tablespoons granulated sugar, if using fresh plums

Vegetable shortening for preparing pan

1/2 (half of 18.25 ounce) box yellow cake mix

Water

1 large egg

Powdered sugar

1 If using fresh plums, cut each in half and remove the seed. Put the halves in a bowl, cover with granulated sugar, and let sit for 30 minutes so the sugar dissolves. If using canned plums, drain off the juice, cut the plums in half and remove the seeds, and set in a bowl while you prepare the batter. (No additional sugar is required.)

2 Preheat the oven according to cake mix directions. Grease 1 (9-inch) cake pan.

3 Mix the cake mix by hand with slightly less than half the water required on the box and only one egg to make a thick batter. Pour into the cake pan. If using fresh plums, drain plums from the dissolved sugar. Arrange the plums on top of the cake batter and bake according to cake box directions or until golden on top.

4 Cool and remove the cake from the pan. Sprinkle powdered sugar on top. Cut in slices and serve.

MAKES 6 TO 8 SERVINGS.

✕✕✕ MOM MOM'S ALMOND TORTE

CAROLINE HODGE (Brentwood, Tennessee) calls her grandma Mom Mom. Mom Mom is CAROLYN JENKINS BOOTH (Nashville, Tennessee), and her favorite thing to do is cook. Caroline shares that they enjoy playing cards together and taking the family's annual summer beach trip, where Mom Mom spends a good part of the week making smoothies and delicious desserts. Another tradition is to get everyone together to celebrate family birthdays, and they can count on Mom Mom to make the celebrant's favorite birthday food—everything from macaroni and cheese to brown rice to cherry cobbler. "Mom Mom has influenced me by teaching me how to serve others with the gifts God has given us. God has given my grandmother the gift of cooking, and she has continued to serve others by taking meals to those who are sick, grieving, or just need encouragement, and she's always willing to make food for parties or when someone has had a baby. I am so thankful she has passed this special gift on to me. I love to cook and help other people. One year Mom Mom, my mom, and I made these almond tortes as Christmas gifts to raise money for a mission trip. Just by selling these delicious and pretty tortes we were able to raise over half of the amount that was needed for the trip," Caroline says.

3/4 cup (1 1/2 sticks) unsalted butter, melted

1 1/2 cups of sugar, plus some for dusting

2 large eggs

1 1/2 teaspoons almond flavoring

1 1/2 cups all-purpose flour

Pinch of salt

1/3 cup thinly sliced or slivered almonds

Sugar for sprinkling on top

---

1 Preheat the oven to 350 degrees. Line a 9- or 10-inch skillet with foil, dull side up.
2 In a large bowl stir together the melted butter and sugar.
3 In a small bowl stir the eggs and almond flavoring; then use a hand mixer on low speed to blend in with the sugar and butter mixture, just until blended. Add the flour and salt and mix on low until well blended. Pour into the prepared skillet.
4 Cover the mixture with sliced almonds. Sprinkle a little sugar on the top. Bake for 30 minutes.

5 Cool completely in the skillet; then carefully lift the torte out of the pan using the sides of the foil. Peel the foil off carefully. Put the torte on a plate to serve or on a board to give away. This is a heavy cake, so cut it into very thin wedges or strips to serve.

MAKES 16 SERVINGS.

NANNY'S COCONUT CRACKER CAKE ✕ ✕ ✕

WELLS GREER CANNON (born in Nashville, Tennessee) is the youngest of six grandchildren for his grandmother, PATSY CANNON (Greenville, South Carolina). Patsy is known as Nanny to her grandkids. In addition to enjoying cooking for her family, Wells shares that Nanny also likes to sew. She made him a very special blanket with cars and trucks on it that he sleeps with every night. She also made him a comfy cushion for the window seat in his bedroom where he now lives, in Castle Rock, Colorado.

Vegetable shortening to prepare pan

32 saltine crackers, crushed

2 cups sugar

2 cups walnuts, chopped

6 large egg whites, beaten stiff

1 (12 ounce) container whipped topping

1 (16 ounce) can crushed pineapple, drained

1/2 cup coconut flakes

1 Preheat the oven to 350 degrees. Grease a 9 x 13-inch baking pan.
2 In a large bowl mix the crackers, sugar, walnuts, and egg whites. Pour into the pan and bake for 25 minutes.
3 Remove from the oven and cool to room temperature. Top with the whipped topping, pineapple, and coconut flakes. Serve immediately or refrigerate.

MAKES 6 TO 8 SERVINGS.

✕✕✕ BUTTERMILK ICED PLUM CAKE

PARTHENIA SHEARON BOYCE lived most of her adult life in Wartrace, Tennessee. Granddaughter MELANIE MARTIN (Nashville, Tennessee) shares that she learned at an early age to eat her "vegetable requirement" at every meal so she could have some of Grandmother's delicious homemade desserts. And she confesses that a few hours later she'd feign hunger, in need of a snack, to beat her brother and daddy to the leftover pie or cake that would be in Grandmother's refrigerator! Melanie adds, "My sweet granddaddy never vied for the leftover desserts—I suppose he knew how much I loved them and made the sacrifice. Plus, Grandmother would make it for him anytime." Melanie shares that this used to be called a prune cake but thinks the name was changed to plum cake to be more appealing.

CAKE:

Vegetable shortening to prepare baking pan

I cup prunes

1/2 cup water

3 large eggs

1 1/2 cups sugar

I cup vegetable oil

I teaspoon vanilla extract

2 cups all-purpose flour

I teaspoon nutmeg

I teaspoon ground cinnamon

I teaspoon allspice

I teaspoon salt

I teaspoon baking soda

I cup buttermilk

1 1/2 cups pecans, chopped

ICING:

1 1/2 cups sugar

1/2 cup (I stick) butter

I cup buttermilk

I tablespoon light corn syrup

1/4 teaspoon baking soda

1 Preheat the oven to 300 degrees. Grease a 9 x 13-inch baking pan.
2 TO MAKE THE CAKE, place the prunes in the water and let them sit until they are plump and easy to mash, approximately 10 minutes. Drain and then mash the prunes with a fork.
3 In a large bowl beat the eggs for two minutes. Add the sugar, oil, and vanilla and mix until well blended.

4 In another large bowl mix the flour, nutmeg, cinnamon, allspice, salt, and baking soda. Add the buttermilk and mix well.

5 Pour the buttermilk mixture into the egg mixture and stir together. Add the pecans and cooled mashed prunes and mix well. Pour into the greased pan. Bake for 40 minutes or until a toothpick inserted in the center comes out clean.

6 To MAKE THE ICING, while the cake finishes baking, place the sugar, butter, buttermilk, corn syrup, and baking soda in a medium saucepan and stir to combine. Over medium-high heat, bring to a slow boil, stirring constantly for approximately 5 minutes. While the cake is still hot, use a toothpick to make holes in the cake, and pour the icing mixture over the cake in the pan. Spread evenly over the top. Cut into squares and serve warm.

MAKES 18 TO 20 SERVINGS.

CHRISTMAS CAKE À LA MARY ╳╳╳

MARY MITCHELL (McMinnville, Tennessee) was born and raised in Centertown, Tennessee, and is known to her grandson as Granny. Mary started a tradition with her daughter, Jennifer Mitchell, that Jennifer is carrying on with her son, **MILES NEELY**. Miles shares that "my mom makes a pretty red and green Jell-O cake every Christmas, just like my Granny did for her when she was growing up." Miles was born in Murfreesboro, Tennessee, and currently lives in Nashville, Tennessee.

Cooking spray and flour for preparing pans

1 (18.25 ounce) box white cake mix, plus ingredients needed to make the cake

1 (3 ounce) box raspberry gelatin

1 (3 ounce) box lime gelatin

2 cups boiling water, divided

1 (9 ounce) container whipped topping

---

1 Preheat the oven based on cake mix directions. Lightly spray and flour two 9-inch round cake pans.

2 Prepare the cake mix as directed on the package. Pour half of the cake batter into each of the pans. Bake the cakes for the amount of time directed on the box. Cool the cakes in the pans for 15 minutes. Poke the cakes with a fork at 1/2-inch intervals.

3 Dissolve each package of gelatin in one cup of the boiling water. Pour the lime gelatin over one cake and the raspberry gelatin over the other cake. Gently remove the cakes from their pans and stack them on a large serving plate. "Ice" the stacked cakes with whipped topping.

4 Chill for 4 hours before serving. Refrigerate any leftovers.

MAKES 10 TO 12 SERVINGS.

LORRAINE'S DOUBLE CHOCOLATE CAKE

GAVIN BOYCE (Nashville, Tennessee) is the first grandchild for his Nana, PATSY BOYCE. Patsy grew up in Centerville, Tennessee, and now lives in Nashville. While Gavin is just four years old, he likes to say that his Nana is one of his best friends. Every Friday she and Papa pick him up, and they play, eat dinner, and go to the park with their two dogs, Junior and Gracy. Nana's recipe was passed down to her from her Mamma, Lorraine Duncan.

CAKE:

Cooking spray and flour for preparing pan

2 cups sugar

2 cups all-purpose flour

4 tablespoons Nestle or other chocolate powdered drink mix

1/2 teaspoon ground cinnamon

1 cup (2 sticks) butter

1 cup water

1/2 cup buttermilk

2 large eggs

1 teaspoon vanilla extract

ICING:

1/2 cup (1 stick) butter

4 tablespoons Nestle or other chocolate powdered drink mix

6 tablespoons whole milk

1 (16 ounce) box powdered sugar

1 teaspoon vanilla extract

1 cup walnuts or pecans, chopped (optional)

1 Preheat the oven to 350 degrees. Lightly spray and flour a 9 x 13-inch baking pan.

2 TO MAKE THE CAKE, in a large bowl mix together the sugar, flour, chocolate drink mix, and cinnamon.

3 In a medium saucepan over high heat, bring the butter and water to a boil. Remove from the heat and pour into the flour mixture. Add the buttermilk, eggs, and vanilla, and mix well. The batter will be thin.

4 Pour the batter into the baking pan and bake for 25 to 30 minutes or until the cake springs back in the center.

5 TO MAKE THE ICING, in a saucepan over medium heat bring the butter, chocolate drink mix, and milk to a boil. Remove from the heat and stir in the powdered sugar, vanilla, and nuts. Pour the icing over the cake while still warm. Allow the cake to cool before serving.

MAKES 18 SERVINGS.

GRANNY'S SKILLET PINEAPPLE UPSIDE-DOWN CAKE ✕✕✕

ANN PACK (Nashville, Tennessee) shares that her grandmother, **GLADYS HIXON**, was known to her grandchildren as Granny. She spent most of her life in Crossville, Tennessee. "Granny was a hard worker who loved the Lord and who also loved to cook! I will never forget her homemade biscuits and how quickly they disappeared. And, if we were lucky enough, she would make chocolate gravy to go with those biscuits. I also remember the hot chocolate she made in the winter . . . hot milk, shaved dark chocolate, sugar, and a dash of salt. So good! Making huge meals for her family was one of the many ways she showed her love. During holidays, the table would be so full of choices that there would barely be a place to sit. There would be two or three choices of meat, every side you could imagine, and several desserts. Granny loved having her family around, and good meals were a way to ensure that would happen," Ann says.

1/4 cup (1/2 stick) butter

1 cup firmly packed brown sugar

1/2 cup chopped pecans

1 (15 ounce) can pineapple slices, undrained

3 large eggs, separated

1 cup sugar

1 cup all-purpose flour

1 teaspoon baking powder

1/2 teaspoon salt

6 to 8 maraschino cherries

---

1 Preheat the oven to 350 degrees.

2 Melt the butter in a 9-inch cast-iron skillet. Add the brown sugar and pecans and stir well.

3 Drain the pineapple, reserving 1/4 cup and 1 tablespoon pineapple juice. Arrange the pineapple rings in a single layer over the brown sugar mixture in the skillet.

4 Beat the egg yolks with a hand mixer at medium speed until thick and lemon colored. Gradually add the sugar, beating well.

5 In a small bowl combine the flour, baking powder, and salt. Add the flour mixture to the yolk mixture. Stir in the reserved pineapple juice.

6 Beat the egg whites at room temperature with a hand mixer until stiff peaks form. Next, fold the egg whites into the batter and stir. Spoon the batter evenly over the pineapple slices.

7 Bake for 40 to 45 minutes. Remove the cake from the oven and let it cool in the skillet for 30 minutes. Gently loosen the edges and turn the cake out of the skillet onto a serving platter. Before serving, drain and place cherries in the center of each pineapple ring.

MAKES 8 SERVINGS.

✕✕✕ NO-BAKE REFRIGERATOR CAKE

JAMEY BOND HAMPTON (Charlotte, North Carolina) remembers that his favorite thing when visiting his grandmother, Maw Maw, CLARIS BOND (Caddo, Alabama), was to wake up early to go down to the barn with her and Paw Paw. He recalls being shocked when he heard the otherwise quiet Maw Maw call the cows to herd them in and out of the barn. The cows used to scare Jamey, so he chose to help gather eggs instead, having the location of each nest memorized. Jamey also remembers people pulling up to the farm to buy their milk and butter and Maw Maw chatting with them for a while; it seemed like a weekly ritual that had to be honored by both parties. When it comes to fond memories of food, there were always fresh biscuits, bacon, ham, or sausage on the stove when they visited. Jamey says he loved Maw Maw's pure country cooking, with all of it tasting even better when it was hot and fresh out of the oven!

---

1 (14 ounce) can evaporated milk	1 (15 ounce) box raisins	2 pounds chopped pecans
1 (16 ounce) bag mini marshmallows	1 (12 ounce) box vanilla wafers, crushed	1 (14 ounce) jar candied fruits
1 cup coconut, shredded or flaked		1/2 teaspoon ground cinnamon

---

1 In a large saucepan add the milk and marshmallows. Heat on medium low, stirring continuously until melted. Add in the coconut, raisins, vanilla wafers, pecans, candied fruits, and cinnamon and mix well.

2 Pour the entire mixture onto a large serving plate and shape into a large loaf. Cover with wax paper and then loosely with foil, and put it into the refrigerator until it is firm. Maw Maw cut it in half once it was firm—one half for slicing and serving, the other half rewrapped and put in an airtight container and returned to the fridge until needed. It can be served cold or left out for several hours. This large loaf is good for a group or for gifting!

MAKES 15 TO 20 SERVINGS.

NOTE: *Regarding the candied fruit—you can use a jar of mixed candied fruit or buy the individual candied fruits that are your favorites, like pineapple or cherries.*

NAMA'S TEXAS SHEET CAKE

Author Faye Porter shares that while her mum, CHARLOTTE LOUISE FERKAN PORTER, isn't from the South, she is a grandma, a great baker, and has kids that live in the South, so we wanted to include her! Charlotte is known as Grandma to older granddaughters and sisters SOPHIA and OLIVIA PORTER. And she is known as Nama to younger granddaughters and sisters AVA and LILLIAN PORTER. Granddaughter Olivia—who also shares her grandmother's middle name, Louise—has a particular love of all things chocolate. Charlotte's husband, four children, and the grandchildren all love this chocolate cake. And it's just as tasty served warm or cold.

CAKE:

Cooking spray

2 cups sugar

2 cups all-purpose flour

1 teaspoon baking soda

1 cup (2 sticks) margarine

4 tablespoons cocoa

1 cup water

2 large eggs

1 teaspoon vanilla extract

1/2 cup buttermilk or sour cream

ICING:

1/2 cup (1 stick) margarine

4 tablespoons cocoa

6 tablespoons buttermilk or milk

3 1/2 cups powdered sugar

1 teaspoon vanilla extract

1 cup chopped pecans (optional)

1 Preheat the oven to 350 degrees. Lightly spray a 15 x 10-inch jelly-roll pan.

2 TO MAKE THE CAKE, mix together the sugar, flour, and baking soda in a large bowl.

3 In a saucepan over medium-high heat, bring the margarine, cocoa, and water to a rapid boil. Pour the cocoa mixture over the flour mixture and blend well. Add the eggs, vanilla, and buttermilk. Mix well. Spread onto the jelly-roll pan.

4 Bake for 15 minutes, checking for doneness with a toothpick.

5 TO MAKE THE ICING, melt the margarine in a saucepan over medium heat. Add the cocoa and buttermilk. Bring to a rapid boil. Stir in the powdered sugar and vanilla. Let the mixture cool slightly, beating every 15 minutes with a wooden spoon until smooth.

6 Stir in the pecans and spread the icing on the warm cake. Serve warm or cool.

MAKES 24 SERVINGS.

NANNY PATSY'S FAVORITE CHOCOLATE SHORTCAKE

WELLS GREER CANNON currently lives in Castle Rock, Colorado, but he was born in Nashville, Tennessee, and lived there until he was about two and a half years old. His Nanny and Papa Cannon live in Greenville, South Carolina, and his Grandma and Grandpa Klehammer live in Franklin, Tennessee. Nanny, PATSY CANNON, just adores Wells—he is the youngest of her six grandchildren. She loves to talk to Wells on the phone and the computer, calling him her "darling." Nanny makes this chocolate shortcake every year for Christmas, and it is a big hit with all the grandchildren!

CAKE:

Vegetable shortening to grease the pan(s)

2 cups all-purpose flour

2 cups sugar

1/2 cup (1 stick) butter

1/2 cup vegetable oil

4 cups cocoa

1 cup water

1/2 cup buttermilk

1 teaspoon vanilla extract

1 teaspoon baking soda

1 teaspoon ground cinnamon

1 teaspoon salt

2 large eggs, slightly beaten

ICING:

2 cups sugar

2/3 cup evaporated milk

1/2 cup (1 stick) unsalted butter

1 (6 ounce) package chocolate chips

1 Preheat the oven to 350 degrees. Grease one 11 x 17-inch pan or three 9-inch round baking pans.

2 TO MAKE THE CAKE, sift together the flour and sugar in a large bowl.

3 In a saucepan over medium-high heat, mix the butter, oil, cocoa, and water. Bring to a boil; then pour over the sugar and flour mixture. Stir well. Add the buttermilk, vanilla, baking soda, cinnamon, salt, and eggs, and mix well. Pour the batter into the pan and bake for 20 minutes.

4 TO MAKE THE ICING, combine the sugar, evaporated milk, and butter in a saucepan and bring to a boil over medium heat. Cook for one minute; then turn off the heat and add the chocolate chips, stirring well until the mixture is smooth. Spread the icing on the warm cake. Serve warm or at room temperature.

MAKES 10 TO 12 SERVINGS.

SANDRA'S STRAWBERRY CAKE

"We always love to eat at Nini's," says grandson **CHRISTIAN STROM** (Bellevue, Tennessee). "She keeps all of the fun snacks on hand that we don't have at home. It's fun to celebrate birthdays or just stay for dinner. No matter the occasion, I love how we are always welcome there." His Nini, **SANDRA MEADOWS** (Nashville, Tennessee), was born in Murfreesboro, Tennessee, and is a grandmother of four. Nini is known for making delicious desserts, and this is one of Christian's favorites. (P.S. Christian adds that the icing is the best part.)

CAKE:

Vegetable shortening and flour to prepare baking pan

1 (10 ounce) package frozen strawberries, thawed

1 (18.25 ounce) box white cake mix

1 (3 ounce) box strawberry gelatin

4 large eggs

1 cup vegetable oil

ICING:

½ cup (1 stick) butter

1 (16 ounce) box powdered sugar

Reserved juice of strawberries

1 Preheat the oven to 350 degrees. Lightly grease and flour a 9 x 13-inch baking pan.

2 **TO MAKE THE CAKE,** drain the thawed berries, being careful to save the juice for the icing.

3 In a large bowl mix together the cake mix, gelatin, eggs, oil, and drained berries. Pour into the baking pan. Bake for the amount of time listed on the cake mix box. The cake is done when a toothpick inserted in the center comes out clean. Remove from the oven and cool on a wire rack.

4 **TO MAKE THE ICING,** in a medium saucepan on low to medium heat, melt the butter. Add the powdered sugar and stir until well blended. Remove from the heat and stir in the strawberry juice. When the cake has cooled, ice and serve.

MAKES 10 TO 12 SERVINGS.

LIZZIE'S ANGEL FOOD CAKE

Mamaw **LISSIE HUGHES** (Abingdon, Virginia) taught through example that if you can help someone, you have an obligation to do so. Granddaughter **MARZETTA FLEMING** (Clintwood, Virginia) believes this value developed so strongly in her Mamaw because she grew up in Clintwood, Virginia, in a very rural, isolated area in the Appalachian Mountains where neighbors and family depended on each other. Marzetta shares that "Mamaw loved baking for her family and friends, and her angel food cake was one of our favorites. Each of her five children had a home within walking distance of Mamaw's, and during our childhoods my cousins and I wore out the paths to her house—especially when she'd call to let us know to hurry on over for warm angel food cake. She was our touchstone, and we all felt very loved and cherished around her. And, of course, we always had Sunday dinner at her house. It's amazing to think back on how much food she served at those dinners—fresh vegetables, deviled eggs, slaws, salads, meat, poultry, rolls, cornbread, and two or three desserts. Most of what she made came straight from her garden or livestock—chickens, milking cows, hogs, etc. She even churned her own butter." Lizzie passed away in 1980.

12 large egg whites	1/4 teaspoon salt	1 3/4 cups sugar
1 teaspoon cream of tartar	1 teaspoon vanilla extract	1 1/4 cups cake flour

1　In a large bowl beat the egg whites with a hand mixer until soft peaks form. Add the cream of tartar, salt, and vanilla to the egg whites. Gradually add the sugar to the mixture while continuing to beat until stiff peaks form.

2　In a separate bowl sift the cake flour four times. Add the sifted cake flour to the egg whites mixture. Pour into an ungreased 10-inch tube cake pan. Place in a cold oven on a lower rack.

3　Turn on the oven to 325 degrees. Bake for 1 hour or until golden brown. Remove from the oven, invert the cake, and allow to cool upside down in the pan for approximately 3 hours. When ready to slice, turn the pan over and run a knife around the edges to loosen before turning the cake over onto a serving dish and slicing.

MAKES 10 TO 12 SERVINGS.

NOTE: *Be careful not to get any egg yolks mixed in with the egg whites. Yolk will prevent the whites from whipping up the way you need them to. Make sure to use cake flour; it's lighter than regular flour. Don't grease your pan, or the cake can fall out when you turn it upside down to cool. Humidity can affect the height of your angel food cake, so plan ahead, and don't bake on a rainy day.*

GRANDMAMA'S POUND CAKE ✕ ✕ ✕

"Isn't that a bird dog?" MARGARET FAYE DAVIS (Memphis, Tennessee) used to say. Margaret was known as Grandmama to granddaughter DEBORAH SURIANI (also of Memphis). Deborah shares that Grandmama was a great cook who made the best food ever—her pound cake, caramel cake, and divinity were particular favorites. "We enjoyed making Christmas candy and chow-chow relish together. From her I learned to love unconditionally and, regardless of what happens, that family is always loved," Deborah adds.

Vegetable shortening and flour to prepare pan

I cup (2 sticks) margarine, softened

I cup (2 sticks) butter, softened

2 cups sugar

2 teaspoons almond extract

2 teaspoons vanilla extract

6 large eggs

2 cups all-purpose flour

2 cups self-rising flour

I cup whole milk

---

1 Preheat the oven to 325 degrees. Grease and flour a tube pan.

2 In a large bowl cream together the margarine, butter, and sugar. Add the almond and vanilla extracts. Add the eggs, one at a time, mixing between each addition. Add the flour alternately with the milk. Mix well after each addition. Pour the cake batter into the pan. Bake for I hour and 45 minutes. Cool before removing from the pan. Slice and serve.

MAKES 10 TO 12 SERVINGS.

GRANNY'S BLACKBERRY CAKE

Even the best cooks have been known to make a mistake, right? BRYAN CURTIS (Nashville, Tennessee) shares that his Granny, IRENE FOSTER (Charlotte, Tennessee), was a wonderful cook. However, there once was this one cake . . . and it ended up being a bit browner than she wanted. So Granny took a knife, attempted to scrape the brown off the top, and actually used her vacuum cleaner to suck up the crumbs! Because Bryan's Uncle Don worked for the Nashville newspaper, there was no "sweeping" this baking blunder under the rug. Uncle Don shared Granny's vacuum story with one of the paper's columnists, and it ended up on the front page! (Thank heavens she had a great sense of humor about it.) Nonetheless, this cake is delicious.

CAKE:

Cooking spray and flour to prepare pans

1 (18.25 ounce) box white cake mix with pudding

1 (3 ounce) box raspberry flavored gelatin

1 cup canola oil

1/2 cup whole milk

4 large eggs

1 cup fresh or frozen blackberries

1 cup sweetened flaked coconut

1 cup pecans, chopped

ICING:

1/2 cup (1 stick) butter, softened

1 pound powdered sugar

1/3 cup milk

3/4 cup fresh or frozen blackberries

1/2 cup sweetened flaked coconut

3/4 cup pecans, chopped

1 Preheat the oven to 350 degrees. Spray and flour 3 (9-inch) cake pans.
2 TO MAKE THE CAKE, in a large bowl combine the cake mix, gelatin, oil, and milk. Combine using a hand mixer on low speed for 1 minute. Add the eggs, beating well after each addition. Fold in the blackberries, coconut, and pecans.
3 Divide the batter between the three cake pans. Bake for 20 to 25 minutes or until the cakes test done. Cool for 5 minutes in the pan. Remove to a wire rack to cool.
4 TO MAKE THE ICING, cream the butter in a large bowl. Add the sugar and milk. Beat until smooth.
5 Fold in the blackberries, coconut, and pecans.

6 TO BUILD THE CAKE: Place one cake layer on a plate and ice the top. Place the second cake on top of the first and ice it. Place the third cake on top and ice the top and sides. Keep leftovers refrigerated.

MAKES 16 SERVINGS.

✕✕✕ CHOCOLATE ÉCLAIR CAKE

"Our grandparents lived just up the hill from my parents in a house they had built from reclaimed log cabins on the property adjacent to ours. We were incredibly fortunate to grow up so close to them, and over the years we enjoyed a lot of Memaw's cooking at birthdays, holidays, and just simple family get-togethers," share brothers **DREW**, **WILL**, and **SETH HELTSLEY** (Tullahoma, Tennessee, recently relocated to California). Memaw is **JANICE COFFMAN EATON** (Tullahoma, Tennessee). Whenever their birthdays rolled around, one of the best parts was getting to choose which type of cake or pie they wanted. Their all-time favorites were Memaw's No-Bake Cheesecake and this Chocolate Éclair Cake.

CAKE:

2 (1 ounce) boxes sugar-free instant vanilla pudding

1 cup powdered sugar

3 cups whole milk

1 (9 ounce) container frozen whipped topping

1 (14.4 ounce) box graham crackers

ICING:

3 tablespoons butter

2 ounces unsweetened chocolate squares

2 tablespoons light corn syrup

1 teaspoon vanilla extract

3 tablespoons whole milk

1 1/2 cups powdered sugar

1 **TO MAKE THE CAKE**, in a large bowl use a hand mixer to combine the pudding, powdered sugar, and milk until thick. Fold in the whipped topping.

2 Cover the bottom of a 9 x 13-inch pan with whole graham crackers. Spread half of the pudding mixture over the crackers. Place another layer of crackers over the pudding; then spread the remaining pudding on top. Add one final layer of crackers.

3 **TO MAKE THE ICING**, melt the butter and chocolate in a small saucepan over medium heat. Add in the corn syrup. Blend in the vanilla, milk, and powdered sugar and mix well. Cool slightly. Spread the entire top with the icing. Refrigerate until ready to serve, and refrigerate any leftovers.

MAKES 10 TO 12 SERVINGS.

GRANDMOTHER'S LEMON CHEESE CAKE

J. Marie Hegler (Mount Juliet, Tennessee) was born in Opp, Alabama, and grew up in Biloxi, Mississippi. She remembers that when growing up, her grandmother, **Corene Botts Hegler Kolman** (Montgomery, Alabama), always seemed so young and hip. She drove a candy apple red car, went out on dates, and loved to travel. Marie says, "She finally 'settled down' again at the end of my freshman year of college when she married her second husband, Ron, who shares her love of travel and enjoys cooking more than she ever did. I guess you could say I have inherited my grandmother's love of books and her love of cakes. We are both insatiable readers, and we both have a terrible sweet tooth. This lemon cheese cake is very different and so delicious. It is a big favorite of my mom's, and even though I am not a big fan of lemony desserts, I love this one. I have no idea why it is called a lemon cheese cake since there is no cheese in it, but that has always been what we've called it since Grandmother referred to the icing as lemon cheese filling."

- 1 (18.25 ounce) box white cake mix, plus ingredients to make cake
- 1 1/2 cups sugar

- 3 tablespoons all-purpose flour
- 1/2 cup lemon juice
- 3 large egg yolks, beaten

- 1 tablespoon butter
- Grated rind of 2 to 3 lemons

---

1 Bake the cake according to the recipe on the box for two round cake pans. Once the cake layers have cooled, carefully slice each layer with a long knife horizontally so that instead of having two thicker layers, you have four thinner ones.

2 Mix the sugar and flour together in the top of a double boiler. (If you don't have a double boiler, use a metal bowl that can sit on top of a pot of boiling water.) Add the lemon juice and beaten egg yolks. Cook over hot water until thick, stirring constantly to prevent lumping.

3 Once the mixture has thickened, remove from the double broiler and stir in the butter and grated lemon rind. Allow to cool. Once cooled, spread over each layer of the cake and over the top and sides of the cake.

MAKES 10 TO 12 SERVINGS.

LEMON SUPREME POUND CAKE ✕ ✕ ✕

ANDREW HELTSLEY (Nashville, Tennessee) lived about three hours from his grand-mother, **HELEN SPARKS NICHOLS** (Greenville, Kentucky), when he was growing up. Helen was known to her grandchildren as MaMaw. Andrew remembers MaMaw hosting large family dinners around her table, and this pound cake was a staple at almost every such event. While this cake was a family favorite, Andrew was especially known for wanting it all to himself. It's super moist and delicious!

CAKE:

Cooking spray and flour to prepare pan

1 (18.25 ounce) box lemon supreme cake mix

1 (3 ounce) box lemon instant pudding mix

1/2 cup vegetable oil

1 cup water

4 large eggs

GLAZE:

1 cup powdered sugar

1 tablespoon plus 1 teaspoon milk or lemon juice

1 teaspoon vegetable oil

1 Preheat the oven to 350 degrees. Spray and flour a 10-inch tube or Bundt pan.

2 **TO MAKE THE CAKE**, in a large bowl use a hand mixer to beat the cake and pudding mix with the oil, water, and eggs for 2 minutes at medium speed. Pour the batter in the pan and bake for 45 to 50 minutes, until the center springs back when touched lightly. Cool 25 minutes in the pan; then invert onto a serving plate.

3 **TO MAKE THE GLAZE**, in a small bowl blend together the powdered sugar, milk, and oil. Spoon over the cake. Slice and serve.

MAKES 10 TO 12 SERVINGS.

✕✕✕ NONNA'S ICED BANANA CAKE

"Whenever, wherever possible, laugh" is some great advice shared by SHIRLEY ANN GALLIMORE MOORE (McKenzie, Tennessee). Shirley was born and raised in Hinkeldale, Tennessee, and is known as Nonna to her three grandsons—LUKE, THOMAS, and DANIEL TYLER (Hendersonville, Tennessee). The boys shared a great story with us about their Nonna's fun nature: They had left some stuffed animals at her house, with strict instructions to take care of them. As a surprise for the boys, the next time they all got together, she took the stuffed animals and seat-belted them in the backseat of her car before driving to meet the family. When Nonna arrived, she was so excited to see the boys and their reaction to her surprise that she locked her keys in the car. A phone call later, a AAA locksmith was peering over his glasses at the buckled-up animals in the backseat, but he didn't say a word. The boys were so tickled to see what good care she had taken of their animals and love to retell this story. This banana cake and yummy icing is a family favorite, with many requesting it from Nonna as their birthday cake of choice.

CAKE:

Vegetable shortening to prepare pan

1 1/2 cups sugar

2 large eggs

2 cups self-rising flour

3 medium ripe bananas

1 1/2 cup chopped walnuts or pecans

1/2 cup (1 stick) butter, melted

ICING:

1 (16 ounce) box powdered sugar

2 medium ripe bananas

1/2 cup (1 stick) butter

1 cup chopped walnuts or pecans

1 Preheat the oven to 350 degrees. Grease a 9 x 13-inch pan.

2 TO MAKE THE CAKE, in a large bowl combine the sugar, eggs, flour, bananas, and walnuts and mix well. Pour the melted butter over the other ingredients and stir well to combine. Pour into the pan.

3 Bake for 30 to 35 minutes or until a toothpick inserted in the middle comes out clean. Allow the cake to cool completely before icing.

4 **To make the icing,** in a medium bowl combine the powdered sugar and bananas and mix well.

5 In a small skillet melt the butter and pour it over the banana mixture. Beat with a hand mixer until smooth, 2 to 3 minutes. Stir in the walnuts. Spread on the cake after it has cooled.

MAKES 12 SERVINGS.

GRANDMOTHER'S POUND CAKE

Debbie McMurtry (Westmoreland, Tennessee) was born in Nashville, Tennessee, but raised in Hendersonville, Tennessee. Debbie is a proud grandma to four grandchildren— two boys and two girls. Grandchildren are **Dustin** and **Jenny McMurtry** (also of Westmoreland) and **Nathaniel** and **Kaylee Stinson** (Scottsville, Kentucky). They share that their Grandma loves to see people eat and that no one ever leaves her house hungry! In fact, Grandma loves to cook so much that she often makes way more food than needed and has to call neighbors to come help them eat it. This recipe is from Debbie's grandmother.

Vegetable shortening and flour to prepare pan	3 cups sugar	$1/2$ teaspoon baking powder
	6 large eggs	
2 sticks butter, softened	3 cups cake flour*	$1/3$ teaspoon salt
	8 ounces heavy whipping cream	1 teaspoon vanilla extract

1 Grease and flour a Bundt pan.

2 In a large bowl use a mixer to cream the butter and sugar together. Add the eggs, one at a time, mixing between each addition. Alternately add the flour and cream, mixing after each addition. Add the baking powder, salt, and vanilla.

3 Pour the batter into the Bundt pan. Place in a cold oven on the middle rack. Heat the oven to 350 degrees, bake for 1 hour, and remove. Let cool before removing from the pan.

MAKES 12 SERVINGS.

* Don't substitute the type of flour.

MOM'S 5-FLAVOR CAKE

ERNIE YOUNG was born in Richmond, Virginia, and now lives in Franklin, Tennessee. Ernie is known as Grammy to her grandchildren. LEXI YOUNG (also in Franklin) was also born in Richmond and is the only granddaughter out of Ernie's four grandchildren. Ernie shares property with Lexi and her family, so they get to spend a lot of quality time together. They enjoy cooking and baking together and attending church on Sundays. This cake is a longtime family favorite, and Ernie receives many requests for it as an honoree's birthday cake of choice.

CAKE:

1/2 cup vegetable shortening, plus extra to prepare pan

1 cup (2 sticks) butter, softened

3 cups sugar

5 large eggs, well beaten

3 cups all-purpose flour, plus extra to prepare pan

1/2 teaspoon baking powder

1 cup milk (whole or 2 percent)

1 teaspoon coconut extract

1 teaspoon butter extract

1 teaspoon lemon extract

1 teaspoon vanilla extract

1 teaspoon rum flavoring

GLAZE:

1 cup sugar

1 teaspoon almond extract

1 teaspoon butter extract

1 teaspoon lemon extract

1 teaspoon vanilla extract

1 teaspoon rum flavoring

1. Preheat the oven to 325 degrees. Grease and flour a 10-inch tube pan.
2. TO MAKE THE CAKE, in a large bowl cream the butter, shortening, and sugar until light and fluffy. Add the eggs and beat until thick and lemon colored, approximately 5 minutes.
3. In a medium bowl combine the flour and baking powder. Alternately add the flour mixture and the milk to the butter mixture. Stir in the coconut, butter, lemon, and vanilla extracts and the rum flavoring.

4 Pour the mixture into the pan and bake 90 minutes or until cake tests done. Remove from the oven and set the pan on a wire rack. Poke a few holes in the cake while it's still warm and before adding the glaze.

5 TO MAKE THE GLAZE, in a heavy saucepan combine the sugar, almond, butter, lemon, and vanilla extracts, and the rum flavoring. Bring to a boil over medium heat and stir until the sugar has melted. Spoon over the warm cake while it is still in the pan. Let the cake sit until it is cool. Once cool, invert to a serving platter. Slice and serve.

MAKES 10 TO 12 SERVINGS.

NANNY'S COCONUT CAKE

"She loved to bake!" remembers ANITA MULLINS (Lexington, Tennessee) "That is one of the main things that comes to my mind when thinking of my grandmother ALMA BELEW (Clarksburg, Tennessee). I remember every Christmas she baked cakes all week long. The same six cakes every year: orange, pineapple, chocolate, jam, banana, and the favorite of all, coconut cake. No canned or bagged coconut though, she only made it from a whole coconut! The milk was used to pour over the cake, and then she shredded the coconut fresh." A homemaker, a farmer's wife, and a mother of four, Grandmother Belew was known to local farm community retailers by her cakes that she made and took around to everyone that they did business with. "Her love of baking has been passed down for three generations, and we all try to recreate her famous cakes each holiday season."

CAKE:

2 1/4 cups flour	I teaspoon salt	3/4 cups shortening
I 1/2 cups sugar	I cup milk	5 egg whites
3 teaspoons baking powder	I 1/2 teaspoon vanilla	I can coconut milk*

SEVEN-MINUTE FROSTING:

3 egg whites	I 1/2 cups sugar	I fresh coconut or I bag sweetened, flaked coconut
5 tablespoons water	1/4 tsp cream of tartar	

1 Preheat the oven to 350 degrees. Grease and flour two round 9-inch cake pans.

2 TO MAKE THE CAKE, in a large bowl combine the flour, sugar, baking powder, and salt. In a medium bowl beat the milk, vanilla, shortening, and egg whites. Add the shortening mixture to the flour mixture and beat with an electric mixer until moistened. Evenly pour the batter into the cake pans and bake for 30 minutes or until a toothpick inserted in the center comes out clear.

3 Allow the cakes to cool in the pan 10 minutes before removing to a wire rack to cool completely.

4 Spoon coconut milk over cake layers and refrigerate. The longer the better, but as long as it soaks in good, you will be able to frost the cake.

5 **TO MAKE THE FROSTING**, combine the egg whites, water, sugar, and cream of tartar in the top pan of a double boiler. Bring water to a boil and place the top pan over the boiling water. Make sure the water doesn't touch the bottom of the top pan. Beat with an electric mixer for seven minutes. Spread the frosting over the cake and sprinkle with coconut. Keep refrigerated until ready to serve. Remove 30 minutes before serving.

MAKES 8 TO 10 SERVINGS.

* You can also use 1 cup milk and $1/2$ cup sugar and bring to a boil and use this if you do not have coconut milk on hand.

Noel Wreaths

Chocolate Chip Cookies

M&M Cookies

Key Lime Cookies

Mimi-Fashioned Tea Cakes

Pumpkin—Chocolate Chip Cookies

Grana's Gooey Butter Cookies

Gran's No-Bake Cookies

Mammy's Old-Fashioned Tea Cakes

Grandpa's Favorite Doodles

Sally's Oatmeal Cookies

✕✕✕ NOEL WREATHS

Every year **SUEANNE KYLE** (Martinsville, Virginia) could hardly wait for the holiday dinners she and her family would have at Nanny **VIRGINIA KESTER'S** (also of Martinsville) house. Sueanne remembers that Nanny's house was filled with the wonderful smell of a roasting turkey and all the trimmings, and there would always be delicious cookies and goodies. Sueanne's favorite cookie was Nanny's Noel Wreaths, and she shares, "I'd make a beeline to the tin as soon as I walked in the door! I'm still traditional, like my Nanny, in that I only make certain cookies at the holidays . . . once they are gone, you won't see them again till the next year. I could always count on the Hickory Farms cheese ball, olives, and spiced apples for appetizers . . . a tradition I still keep for my holidays. And we always dressed up for those dinners." (Sueanne now lives in Marlborough Massachusetts.)

1 cup (2 sticks) butter, softened	1 teaspoon vanilla extract	1 1/3 cups roasted pecans, chopped
1/2 cup sugar	2 1/2 cups all-purpose flour, plus extra for rolling out dough	1/4 cup maple syrup
1 large egg		Red and green candied cherries, cut into pieces

1 In a large bowl use a hand mixer to beat the butter and sugar until fluffy, about 4 minutes. Add the egg and vanilla. Stir in the flour in three batches, blending after each addition, to make a soft dough.

2 In a small bowl take one-third of the dough and mix with the pecans and maple syrup.

3 Put the rest of the dough in the refrigerator for 4 hours. When dough is ready, preheat the oven to 350 degrees.

4 Roll dough on a lightly floured surface, and use a cookie cutter to cut the dough into circular shapes. Drop 1/2 teaspoon of the nut filling onto the middle of each cookie and add a piece of candied cherry at the top for the "bow." Bake on a cookie sheet lined with parchment paper or a nonstick baking sheet for 10 to 12 minutes, just until golden brown.

5 Let the cookies cool on the baking tray for 2 minutes, and then transfer to a wire rack to cool completely. Store in an airtight container (a holiday tin is beautiful) and keep in a cool, dry place. Will keep for two months. Nanny's recipe card says it makes a "tin full!"

MAKES 6 DOZEN COOKIES.

CHOCOLATE CHIP COOKIES ✕ ✕ ✕

REESE ELIZABETH SHEFFIELD (Nashville, Tennessee) is the second of two grand-daughters of Grandma KATHLEEN GANDY SHEFFIELD. While Kathleen was born in White Settlement, Texas, she now lives in Nashville, Tennessee. Reese and big sister Isabel share that Grandma's chocolate chip cookies are their absolute favorite! Grandma frequently makes these for the girls, and they are their "prize" to be earned when they eat a good supper. Grandma received this recipe from a fellow army wife when PawPaw was stationed at Fort Sill, Oklahoma.

1 cup (2 sticks) margarine, softened

1 cup vegetable oil

1 1/2 cups sugar

1 1/2 cups brown sugar

2 large eggs

2 teaspoons vanilla extract

1 tablespoon water

1 (12 ounce) package semisweet chocolate chips

5 1/2 cups all-purpose flour

2 teaspoons baking soda

1 teaspoon salt

1/2 chopped walnuts (optional)

1 Preheat the oven to 350 degrees.

2 In a large bowl use a hand mixer to cream the margarine, oil, sugar, and brown sugar together. Add the eggs, vanilla, water, chocolate chips, flour, baking soda, salt, and walnuts, and mix well. (Kathleen lets the dough sit in the refrigerator overnight so it is are a lot easier to handle the next day.) Drop by teaspoonfuls, onto ungreased cookie sheets. Bake for 10 to 12 minutes.

MAKES APPROXIMATELY 4 DOZEN COOKIES.

Twin sisters LESLIE YOUNG and KAYLA YOUNG THOMPSON (Franklin, Tennessee) remember going to church with their grandparents and eating dinner with them every Sunday when they were growing up. After dinner, they would play games, go shopping, shoot baskets, go sledding in the winter, or make cookies with their grandmother, NANCY BURKE (also of Franklin). The girls share that these cookies were always their favorite. "While Grandmother let us eat all the cookie dough we wanted, we always seemed to have enough left over to bake some cookies," they add. And Grandmother loves these because they are so easy to make.

I (18.25 ounce) box cake mix (yellow, chocolate, or your favorite flavor)

½ cup vegetable oil

2 large eggs

1 ½ cups M&M candies

1 Preheat the oven to 350 degrees.

2 In a large bowl stir the cake mix, oil, and eggs together. Mix in the candy. Spoon little balls of dough onto an ungreased cookie sheet. Bake for 8 minutes. Check for doneness at 6 to 7 minutes, and be sure not to overbake.

MAKES APPROXIMATELY 48 COOKIES.

⟨×⟩× KEY LIME COOKIES

MYRTLE TRULL was affectionately known as Mamaw to her grandchildren. Mamaw was born and raised in Humboldt, Tennessee, and later lived in Jackson, Tennessee. Granddaughter MELODY BARLOW (Murfreesboro, Tennessee) recalls that Sunday dinner was always fried chicken and roast beef with potatoes and carrots, other fresh vegetables, and cantaloupe, when it was in season. "I loved her egg custard pie and tea cakes that were thick, soft sugar cookies," Melody adds.

Cooking spray

1/2 cup lime juice or juice from 3 Key limes

1 large egg

1/2 cup vegetable oil

1 (18.25 ounce) box lemon cake mix

---

1 Preheat the oven to 350 degrees. Lightly spray a cookie sheet.

2 In a large bowl add the lime juice and egg and beat with a fork. Add the oil and cake mix and cream together with an electric mixer.

3 Scoop out by teaspoonfuls onto a cookie sheet, and place 2 inches apart. Bake for 10 to 12 minutes. Watch carefully, as these will burn easily. Cool on a wire rack before serving.

MAKES APPROXIMATELY 1 1/2 DOZEN COOKIES.

MIMI-FASHIONED TEA CAKES

JOSH STANDIFER (Cleveland, Tennessee) remembers the holidays always being a huge deal with his grandmother, Mimi, HELON BARRON STANDIFER (Dothan, Alabama). And Christmas was the best! Mimi started cooking way before December 25 to ensure all her precious treats were made to perfection. "I will always remember the smell of walking into her house. The aroma of the wonderful things she was baking filled the air as if to warmly invite us into the 'wonderland' that was Mimi's house and Christmas," Josh adds.

- 2 1/2 cups all-purpose flour, plus extra for rolling out dough
- 2 teaspoons baking powder
- 1 cup sugar
- 1/2 cup (1 stick) butter, softened
- 1 large egg
- 1/2 cup whole milk
- 1 teaspoon vanilla extract
- Vegetable shortening for preparing cookie sheets

---

1 Sift the flour and baking powder into a bowl.
2 In a separate bowl cream together the sugar and butter. Add the egg and beat well. Add the flour mixture alternately with the milk and vanilla. Mix all together and cover. Chill in the refrigerator for 2 hours.
3 Preheat the oven to 350 degrees. Grease 2 cookie sheets.
4 On a lightly floured surface, roll the dough thin, approximately 1/4 inch thick. Cut with a small round cookie cutter and place on prepared cookie sheets. Bake until lightly brown, approximately 6 to 8 minutes. Cool on wire racks before serving. Enjoy your tea cakes with Mimi's Hot Tea on page 4.

MAKES 1 1/2 DOZEN COOKIES.

NOTE: *You can try other cookie flavors by replacing the vanilla extract with lemon or almond extract.*

PUMPKIN-CHOCOLATE CHIP COOKIES ✕ ✕ ✕

ANN WILLHOIT (Ruther Glen, Virginia) is one of five granddaughters for Grammy, ESTHER ELAINE FERKAN GREGG (Lexington, Kentucky). Ann loves that every time they visited, Grammy would retell the story of Ann's older sister, Leigh, as a little girl. They were eating lunch one day at a local café, and all the other women remarked about how cute Leigh was, even offering items off their lunch plates to her. There was one woman who didn't offer anything, and Leigh looked at her and said, "Grammy, she's not sharing!" That one line became such a funny saying growing up, and Leigh and Ann still laugh about the story to this day. They miss Grammy, who passed away in 2008.

Vegetable shortening to prepare cookie sheets

1/2 cup (1 stick) margarine, softened

1 1/2 cups sugar

1 cup canned solid-pack pumpkin

1 large egg, beaten to blend

1 teaspoon vanilla extract

2 1/2 cups all-purpose flour

1 teaspoon baking soda

1 teaspoon baking powder

1 teaspoon ground cinnamon

1 teaspoon nutmeg

1/2 teaspoon salt

1 (6 ounce) package semisweet chocolate chips

1/2 cup chopped walnuts (optional)

1 Preheat the oven to 350 degrees. Lightly grease 2 cookie sheets.

2 In a large bowl use a hand mixer to cream together the margarine and sugar until fluffy. Blend in the pumpkin, egg, and vanilla.

3 In a medium bowl sift the flour, baking soda, baking powder, cinnamon, nutmeg, and salt.

4 Add the flour mixture to the margarine mixture and blend well. Stir in the chocolate chips and nuts. Drop the batter by heaping teaspoons onto the prepared cookie sheets.

5 Bake until lightly brown, about 12 to 15 minutes. Cool on a wire rack before serving. Store leftovers in an airtight container.

MAKES 2 DOZEN COOKIES.

GRANA'S GOOEY BUTTER COOKIES

Grandchildren LOLA, ABE, MAGGIE, and ELIZA (Lebanon, Tennessee) and ADDIE, ELENA, and CHLOE (Murfreesboro, Tennessee) say their Grana, ALISON FRANCESCA COLLIER (Mount Juliet, Tennessee), lets them help bake these delicious cookies and, of course, eat the dough and lick the bowl and spoons. One of their favorite things to do is have sleepovers at Grana and Poppy's because the next morning usually means pancakes and chocolate milk. They each get to pick their favorite shape from her special box of cookie cutters, and when Grana cooks the pancakes, they make their cut-outs. They can all recite Grana's "three important things to remember" when making the perfect cut-out—press, twist, and pull! Grana is also teaching them to trust in the Lord, as He knows all and sees all. She hopes they will always try to look for the good in people and be kind.

1 (8 ounce) package cream cheese, softened

1/2 cup (1 stick) butter, softened

1 large egg

1/4 teaspoon vanilla extract

1 (18.25 ounce) box yellow cake mix

1/4 cup powdered sugar

1 Preheat the oven to 350 degrees.

2 In a large bowl use a hand mixer to cream together the cream cheese and butter. Stir in the egg and vanilla. Add the dry cake mix. Stir until all the ingredients are well blended.

3 Spray your hands with cooking spray and roll the dough into 1-inch balls. Roll the balls in the powdered sugar and place 1 inch apart on an ungreased cookie sheet.

4 Bake for 10 to 13 minutes until lightly browned on the bottom. Leave the cookies on the cookie sheet to cool on a wire rack. Once the cookies have cooled, remove them from the cookie sheet.

MAKES APPROXIMATELY 4 DOZEN COOKIES.

NOTE: *It's very important to keep your hands sprayed with cooking spray to keep the dough from sticking to your fingers. You can also try this same recipe with any flavor of cake mix and added flavoring to give the cookies a little zest!*

GRAN'S NO-BAKE COOKIES ✕ ✕ ⟩

AVERY CLAIRE HAMPTON (Mount Juliet, Tennessee) and her Gran, SHERRY BOND HAMPTON (Caddo, Alabama), have always been close, and they share a strong love for animals. Gran currently has three cats—all of whom were strays that just happened to show up when Avery and her brother, Cade, were visiting. Both Gran and Avery are no-nonsense gals who don't spend a lot of time on hair or makeup—though they do like the occasional nail-painting session. Just like these women, these no-bake cookies are no fuss and a hit at every family function. In fact, they're now such a tradition, the family doesn't even have to ask Gran to bring them anymore; it's just expected. "If Gran were to show up without them, we'd know she was out of peanut butter," says Avery.

3 tablespoons cocoa

1/2 cup whole milk

1/2 cup (1 stick) butter

1 teaspoon vanilla extract

2 cups sugar

1/3 teaspoon salt

1/2 cup peanut butter

3 cups rolled oats

1 In a saucepan combine the cocoa, milk, butter, vanilla, sugar, and salt and bring to a low boil over medium heat, stirring continuously. Boil for 1 minute. Remove from the heat.

2 Add the peanut butter and oats and mix well. Drop by spoonfuls onto wax paper. Allow to cool completely and harden before eating. Store tightly covered at room temperature.

MAKES 2 DOZEN COOKIES.

❬✕❭✕ MAMMY'S OLD-FASHIONED TEA CAKES

SALLY LANGSTON (Saltillo, Mississippi) was known as Mammy to her twenty-plus grandchildren. She made these old-fashioned tea cakes several times a month but always had trouble keeping her grandkids out of the dough because it was so delicious. This treasured family favorite was passed on to her daughter, Erma Langston Smith, who in turn passed it on to her four daughters: SARAH SMITH, MARY NELL MILLWOOD, BARBARA COWAN (all of Tupelo, Mississippi), and NANCY McGEE (Murfreesboro, Tennessee). It continues to be enjoyed by multiple generations of fans.

5 ½ cups all-purpose flour, plus extra for rolling out the dough

2 cups sugar

½ teaspoon salt

¾ cup vegetable shortening or lard, plus extra to prepare pan

I teaspoon baking soda

2 large eggs

I cup buttermilk

2 ½ teaspoons hot water

I teaspoon vanilla extract

Sugar to sprinkle

1 In a large bowl blend the flour, sugar, salt, and shortening.
2 In a small bowl dissolve the baking soda in hot water.
3 In a medium bowl add the eggs and buttermilk, the baking soda mixture, and hot water. Mix well. Add the vanilla and combine with the flour mixture. Mix well. Chill the dough in the refrigerator for 1 hour.
4 Preheat the oven to 425 degrees. Grease a cookie sheet with shortening.
5 On a lightly floured surface, roll the dough out to ¼-inch thickness. Using a small biscuit cutter or cookie cutter, cut into desired shapes. Sprinkle the tops with granulated sugar and place on cookie sheets approximately 1 ½ inches apart. Bake for 8 to 10 minutes until very lightly browned. Allow to cool 5 minutes on the cookie sheets before moving to a wire rack.

MAKES APPROXIMATELY 4 ½ DOZEN COOKIES.

NOTE: *It's important to roll these thin or they will swell up too thick. Be careful not to overbake, or they will get too hard. While Mammy only used vanilla, you can add other flavoring—orange, almond, lemon—to change it up a bit. Or try adding some food coloring to change the dough color for the holidays.*

GRANDPA'S FAVORITE DOODLES

EILEEN SHERRILL (Peachtree City, Georgia) was born and raised in Port Arthur, Texas. She is known as Gran to her three grandchildren, for whom she's created a number of handmade quilts. She is a retired kindergarten teacher who loves to share books and story time with the little ones. Grandson GRADY MASON'S (Nashville, Tennessee) mom and aunt love to cook and bake with Gran. It's been a tradition for Gran to make these cookies every year for Christmas, as they were her father-in-law's absolute favorites! Now Grady's mom makes them and is proud that this treasured family favorite is being passed on to a new generation. The family affectionately calls the cookies "Grandpa's Favorite Doodles" in honor of him. Grady looks forward to growing up and helping his Gran in the kitchen one day soon.

I cup vegetable shortening

I 1/2 cups plus 2 tablespoons sugar, divided

2 large eggs

2 3/4 cups all-purpose flour

2 teaspoons cream of tartar

I teaspoon baking soda

1/2 teaspoon salt

2 teaspoons ground cinnamon

---

1 In a large bowl use a hand mixer to cream together the shortening and I 1/2 cups of the sugar. Add the eggs and mix well.

2 In another large bowl sift together the flour, cream of tartar, baking soda, and salt. Add to the creamed mixture and mix well. Chill the dough for 60 minutes.

3 Preheat the oven to 400 degrees.

4 Mix the remaining 2 tablespoons of sugar and cinnamon together in a shallow dish. Roll the dough into I-inch balls and roll them in the cinnamon-sugar mixture. Place the balls on an ungreased cookie sheet 2 inches apart. Bake until barely brown but still soft, about 8 minutes. Remove from the oven and place the cookies on a wire rack to cool.

MAKES APPROXIMATELY 4 DOZEN COOKIES.

NOTE: *Don't overbake or the cookies will dry out.*

SALL'S OATMEAL COOKIES

S ALLY L ANGSTON (Saltillo, Mississippi) was known as Mammy to her twenty-plus grandchildren. It seemed as if she was always cooking and baking delicious cookies and cakes, and according to her family, "Mammy never needed a special occasion to bake!" These oatmeal cookies were a particular favorite of now-grown grandsons J OE and B OB S MITH (both of Tupelo, Mississippi), and as long as she had the ingredients in the house, they could expect to delight in these cookies anytime they visited her.

Vegetable shortening
for preparing
cookie sheets

2 cups rolled oats,
uncooked

3 large eggs

I $1/3$ cups sugar

I teaspoon baking
powder

2 teaspoons vanilla
extract

2 tablespoons butter,
melted

$1/4$ cup raisins,
coconut, or nuts
(optional*)

---

1 Preheat the oven to 375 degrees. Grease 2 cookie sheets.

2 In a large bowl combine the oats, eggs, sugar, baking powder, vanilla, butter, and raisins. Stir to combine. Drop by $1/2$ teaspoonfuls onto the greased cookie sheets. Bake for 10 minutes or until the cookies are brown around the edges.

MAKES APPROXIMATELY 2 $1/2$ DOZEN COOKIES.

* If you decide to add the optional raisins, coconut, or nuts, start with $1/4$ cup and then add more to your liking.

Granny's Caramel Icing

Blond Brownies

Nana's Old-Fashioned Egg Custard

MawMaw's Divinity

Marshmallow Cream Fudge

Grandma Clanton's Ice Cream

Ding Bats

Granny's Chess Squares

Geri's Chocolate Pudge

Franklin Famous Cake Balls

Mammy's Blueberry Yum Yum

Cornersville Cracker Treats

Memaw's No-Bake Cheesecake

Chattanooga Chew-Chews (a.k.a. Turtles)

Special Surprise "Dirt Cake"

Glenna's Grandma's Apple Dumplings

Chocolate Coconut Balls à la Nini

Carolina Peanut Butter Candy

Sweet Potato Dessert Pudding

Hello Dollies

Pineapple Casserole

Granny's Bear Wiggle Delight

Honey's Peanut Brittle

Miscellaneous
Desserts

GRANNY'S CARAMEL ICING

This caramel icing recipe is a favorite among Granny MARY JANE CRABTREE'S (Wynne, Arkansas) grandchildren. And, remembers granddaughter ANGIE CRABTREE REYNOLDS (Nashville, Tennessee), there was always a cake on her Granny's kitchen counter. Even though Granny used a store-bought angel food cake, it is the icing that brings back fond memories for all of us. Angie shares, "As I looked through our family cookbook to submit this recipe, I noticed a lot of the recipes included Pet milk. I asked my dad about this. He said it's because they only had an icebox, and space inside would be at a premium, so they used a lot of canned evaporated milk. It is the evaporated milk that really makes this different from any other caramel icing. It gives it a distinct flavor."

3 cups sugar

1 1/4 cups evaporated milk

1/4 cup (1/2 stick) butter

1 teaspoon vanilla extract

1 cup finely chopped pecans (optional)

1 (10 inch) prepared angel food cake

1 In a heavy saucepan bring the sugar, milk, and butter to a boil. Boil 3 minutes, stirring constantly. Cook and stir until the mixture begins to thicken. Remove from the heat and add the vanilla and pecans, if desired. Pour over the angel food cake and let sit until the icing sets.

MAKES ENOUGH TO ICE ONE 10-INCH CAKE.

BLOND BROWNIES ✕ ✕ ✕

While SUEANNE KYLE now lives in Marlborough Massachusetts, her roots are in Martinsville, Virginia. Sueanne shares that her Nanny, VIRGINIA KESTER (also of Martinsville), was the quintessential genteel Southern lady . . . welcoming you into her beautiful home with phlox blooming beautifully on the front bank and serving you a glass of freshly brewed sweet iced tea with homemade cookies. She was always impeccably dressed, even when she was doing yard work! Sueanne says, "Even though I now live in New England, I'd like to think I'm still that Southern lady my Nanny taught me to be." Nanny passed away in 1992.

Vegetable shortening and flour to prepare pan

1/2 cup (I stick) butter, melted

2 cups firmly packed light brown sugar

2 tablespoons water

2 large eggs

2 teaspoons vanilla extract

2 1/3 cups all-purpose flour

I teaspoon baking powder

1/4 teaspoon baking soda

I teaspoon salt

I cup roasted chopped pecans

I (12 ounce) package bittersweet chocolate chips

1 Preheat the oven to 350 degrees. Grease and flour a 9 x 13-inch pan.

2 In a large bowl use a hand mixer to combine the butter, brown sugar, and water. Beat in the eggs, one at a time, and then add the vanilla.

3 In a medium bowl mix the flour with the baking powder, baking soda, and salt. Slowly add the flour mixture to the butter mixture and beat to combine. Stir in the pecans.

4 Pour the batter into the pan. Sprinkle the chocolate chips on top and lightly press them into the batter with the heel of your hand.

5 Bake for 30 minutes. Let cool in the pan for 30 minutes, and then cut into squares. Can be stored in an airtight container or a refrigerator for a week.

MAKES 18 SQUARES.

⟨X⟩ NANA'S OLD-FASHIONED EGG CUSTARD

ELLEN OGLESBY MAYS (Nana) was born in Pennsylvania in 1889, raised in Sparrows Point on the Chesapeake Bay in Baltimore County, Maryland, and in her later years lived in Asheville, North Carolina. When granddaughter ARLENE RAINES (Goodlettsville, Tennessee) was preparing to marry, Nana quoted Ephesians 4:26 about not letting the sun go down on your anger and told Arlene if she followed that advice she would most likely have a very happy marriage. Arlene adds, "While I haven't always followed her advice, I've never forgotten it, and my husband and I have been happily married for more than forty-two years now." Nana was concerned about healthful living and was always looking for new, healthy recipes. She was interested in vegetarian cooking long before it was in vogue. Her old-fashioned egg custard recipe, given to Arlene in 1980, was handwritten on the back of a page from a *Diet and Exercise* magazine containing vegetarian recipes.

2 2/3 cups whole milk	1/2 teaspoon salt	1/2 teaspoon nutmeg
4 large eggs	I teaspoon vanilla	
2/3 cup brown sugar	extract or almond flavoring	

1 Preheat the oven to 450 degrees.
2 In a medium saucepan heat the milk over medium heat until tiny bubbles form around the edges of the pan. Be careful not to burn.
3 In a medium bowl beat the eggs and sugar and add the scalded milk slowly while continuing to stir. Add the salt, vanilla, and nutmeg and stir until all is dissolved.
4 Pour into custard cups or a large baking pan. Set the custard cups or baking pan in a large pan of water. The water should come up at least halfway on the cups or dish. Bake for about 15 minutes or a little longer. Watch it, because it does not take long. Use a table knife to test. When the knife comes out clean, it is done. Refrigerate and serve cold.

MAKES 4 TO 6 SERVINGS.

WILDA DOWNEY DEDRICK w[...] Mobile, Alabama, until she p[...] around and being silly with th[...] Tennessee), "I think I get so[...] mom (Gwen Dedrick McCo[...] ity. She would make them an[...] of it to try when my mom w[...]

2 ½ cups sugar

½ cup light corn syrup

½ cup water

1 Combine the sugar, corn syrup, and water in a medium saucepan. Heat to boiling over medium heat, stirring constantly. Continue to cook, without stirring, until a candy thermometer reaches 260 degrees. Test for the hard ball stage by dropping a teaspoon of syrup into a cup of cold water.

2 When the syrup is almost at the desired temperature, beat the egg whites in a large bowl until stiff. While beating constantly, slowly pour the syrup into a large bowl in a thin stream over the egg whites. Beat until the mixture holds its shape and looks non-glossy. Beat in the vanilla.

3 When the mixture is cool, stir in the nuts and cherries and drop by teaspoonfuls onto a cookie sheet. Allow to set for 20 minutes before serving.

MAKES 16 SERVINGS.

NOTE: *Divinity can be sensitive to high humidity. It's best to make it when the humidity is low.*

MARSHMALLOW CREAM FUDGE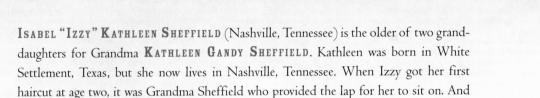

ISABEL "IZZY" KATHLEEN SHEFFIELD (Nashville, Tennessee) is the older of two grand-daughters for Grandma KATHLEEN GANDY SHEFFIELD. Kathleen was born in White Settlement, Texas, but she now lives in Nashville, Tennessee. When Izzy got her first haircut at age two, it was Grandma Sheffield who provided the lap for her to sit on. And Grandma shares that she has a video of Izzy singing "Happy birthday" to her that she will always treasure—she looks forward to playing it for Izzy when she's old enough to get a little embarrassed. Isabel's middle name is after her Grandma Kathleen.

Butter to prepare pan

3 cups sugar

1 cup evaporated milk

6 tablespoons margarine

1 (12 ounce) package chocolate chips

1 (7 ounce) jar marshmallow cream

1 cup chopped pecans (optional)

1 Grease a 9 x 9-inch pan.
2 In a medium saucepan mix the sugar, milk, and margarine together and cook over medium heat until the mixture comes to a boil, stirring frequently. Boil for 5 minutes, stirring constantly.
3 Remove from the heat and stir in the chocolate chips and marshmallow cream. An electric mixer may be used to blend. Add nuts if desired. Pour into the pan. Allow to cool and set before serving. Store in the refrigerator.

MAKES 16 FUDGE SQUARES.

✕✕✕ GRANDMA CLANTON'S ICE CREAM

"Freezing ice cream has been a tradition in our family for many years," shares TAMMY GIBSON (Springfield, Tennessee). And that tradition started with her Grandma Clanton, HESTER ANN LYBARGER FRY CLANTON (Salisbury, Missouri). "We would visit Grandma Clanton, and she would always have treats for us. As children, two of my brothers, Earl and Bobby, had birthdays in July. We celebrated with fireworks and homemade ice cream—quite a combination! To this day, I still request ice cream when I go home. Thank goodness my mother carries on Grandma's tradition. Everyone takes a turn cranking the freezer, and the lucky ones get to lick the paddle," she adds.

---

3 ½ cups sugar

1 cup all-purpose flour

1 cup plus one gallon whole milk, divided

5 large eggs, beaten

1 (8 ounce) container sour cream

½ teaspoon baking soda

1 (14.5 ounce) can sweetened condensed milk

1 teaspoon vanilla extract

---

1 In a medium saucepan cook the sugar, flour, 1 cup of the milk, and eggs over medium heat until thickened.

2 In a small bowl add the sour cream and then stir in the baking soda and set aside while cooking the custard. Let the custard cool and then add the sweetened condensed milk, vanilla, and sour cream mixture.

3 Add the gallon of milk to the mixture and blend all together.

4 Pour into a 6-quart (1.5 gallon) ice-cream freezer. Freeze in the ice-cream freezer or hand crank in an old-fashioned freezer according to manufacturer's directions or until firm.

MAKES 6 QUARTS OR 1.5 GALLONS.

DING BATS ✕ ✕ ✕

Grandson GRAY MCCOY (Hermitage, Tennessee) shares, "One year my MawMaw, WILDA DOWNEY DEDRICK (Mobile, Alabama), bought me the coolest play kitchen for Christmas. We spent the whole day 'cooking' and 'baking' good stuff for my mom and dad in that new little kitchen. I even had an awesome apron with a train on it. At bath time MawMaw would fill the tub with lots of bubbles and then tell me to be sure and wash the 'tater rolls' on my neck. I'm still not sure what a tater roll is, but I hope it's clean." MawMaw's mother-in-law had a HUGE pecan tree in her yard, so MawMaw always had a freezer full of pecans ready for baking. These ding bats were her favorite candy to make at the holidays to give to neighbors, friends, and anyone else who needed a treat. We have no idea why she called them ding bats—maybe because you could eat them till you're batty?" Wilda passed away in 2007.

3/4 cup (1 1/2 sticks) margarine

1 cup sugar

1 (8 ounce) package chopped dates, pitted

1 teaspoon vanilla extract

2 cups crispy rice cereal

1 cup chopped pecans

1 (16 ounce) box powdered sugar

1 Melt the margarine in a medium saucepan over low heat. Add the sugar and dates and cook over low heat, stirring occasionally, until the dates are dissolved (or clear), 5 to 8 minutes. Remove from the heat.

2 Add the vanilla, rice cereal, and pecans. Mix well. Set aside to cool—the mixture can be warm to the touch but not hot.

3 Shape into Ping-Pong-size balls, and then roll in powdered sugar. Chill in the refrigerator approximately 40 minutes before serving.

MAKES ABOUT 50 BALLS.

XXX GRANNY'S CHESS SQUARES

How many people can say that their Granny has their back? JESSICA DILLARD (Lewisburg, Tennessee) says hers does! LINDA ORR (Kingston Springs, Tennessee) has always told Jessica that she supports her in whatever she does and has taught her to be a strong, independent woman who can do whatever she sets her mind to. Jessica's favorite day of the year is December 25 because her family goes to Granny's for Christmas breakfast. Well, it's actually more like a Christmas feast! Granny works so hard to make sure everything is perfect, and the spread is on the table waiting as soon as the family walks in. And, Jessica shares, "Of course, it is always perfect. Then we spend the rest of the day opening presents and watching and quoting from *A Christmas Story* while trying to contain our laughter. It's always so much fun, and it warms my heart to get to spend all day with Granny, the most caring and tenderhearted woman I know."

Cooking spray

1 (18.25 ounce) box yellow cake mix with pudding

4 large eggs, divided

½ cup (1 stick) margarine, melted

1 (8 ounce) package cream cheese, softened

1 (16 ounce) box powdered sugar

---

1 Preheat the oven to 350 degrees. Spray a 9 x 13-inch glass pan.

2 In a medium bowl mix the cake mix, 1 egg, and margarine together and press into the pan.

3 In a medium bowl use a hand mixer to combine the cream cheese, powdered sugar, and remaining 3 eggs and mix well. Pour on top of the first layer.

4 Bake for 45 minutes or until golden brown on top.

MAKES 12 SERVINGS.

GERI'S CHOCOLATE PUDGE ✕ ✕ ✕

When oldest grandson **J. J. DUBIN** (Nashville, Tennessee) was about eighteen months old, his grandma, **GERI WASKIEWICZ** (Spring Hill, Tennessee), shared a piece of her homemade fudge with him at Christmastime. Minutes later J. J. raced into the kitchen, frantically reaching up to the counter, demanding more of her delicious "pudge." To this day, he still refers to Grandma's homemade fudge as "pudge," and it tickles her every time she hears it.

Cooking spray

4 ½ cups sugar

1 (14.5 ounce) can evaporated milk (unsweetened)

1 cup (2 sticks) butter

4 cups semisweet chocolate chips

1 (7 ounce) jar marshmallow cream

2 teaspoons vanilla extract

2 ½ cups chopped walnuts or pecans (optional)

1 Lightly spray a 9 x 13-inch pan.

2 In a large pot add the sugar and milk and stir over medium heat. Bring to a boil and stir constantly until the mixture reaches 240 degrees on a candy thermometer.

3 Place the butter in a large bowl and pour the hot mixture over it. Add the chocolate chips and marshmallow cream and beat on low speed for 5 minutes. Add the vanilla and nuts and mix well.

4 Pour into the pan. When cooled to room temperature, cut into bite-size pieces. Keep leftovers tightly covered; it does not need to be refrigerated.

MAKES 5 POUNDS; APPROXIMATELY 72 BITE-SIZE PIECES.

FRANKLIN FAMOUS CAKE BALLS ✕✕✕

DAVID PAGE (Franklin, Tennessee) was born in Nashville, Tennessee. His grandmother is CAROLYN BOOTH (also of Nashville), who is affectionately known to her grandchildren as Mom Mom. Mom Mom makes these cake balls and does all kinds of variations with them. David submitted this version, though, because it's his personal favorite. Mom Mom uses different kinds of cake mixes for the actual cake balls—sometimes orange, sometimes yellow. And sometimes she uses white chocolate bark to decorate them extra pretty. David shares, "Of course, Mom Mom likes them to look nice on the table, but all I care about is eating them. My brother and I love to make them with her, but they don't last long enough to worry about making them pretty! When I had my high school graduation party, Mom Mom made a beautiful tray of these delicious cake balls. They were a HUGE hit, and everyone thought they came from a bakery. These were a lot better than bakery-bought since they were made with lots of love from Mom Mom."

1 (18.25 ounce) box chocolate cake mix, plus ingredients to make cake	1 (14 ounce) can sweetened condensed milk	1 (16 ounce) package chocolate bark or any sweetened, meltable chocolate

1 Preheat the oven according to cake mix package directions.

2 Prepare the cake according to package directions and bake in a 9 x 13-inch pan as directed on the box. Let the cake cool completely.

3 When the cake is cool, crumble it into a bowl and pour the can of sweetened condensed milk over the cake and mix it with your hands. Cover and place in the refrigerator to chill overnight.

4 Roll small cake balls by hand, about the size of a Ping-Pong ball or golf ball and place on wax paper.

5 Melt the chocolate using a double boiler or microwave. (If using a microwave, put a cup at a time in a microwave-safe bowl, heat 45 seconds, and stir. If it needs to melt further, do so in increments of 30 additional seconds at a time until it is smooth. Trying to melt too quickly or for too long will make the chocolate taste scorched and have a grainy appearance.) Dip the balls into the melted chocolate. Place on wax paper to dry. Serve when the chocolate is set. Refrigerate leftovers in an airtight container.

MAKES APPROXIMATELY 3 DOZEN CAKE BALLS.

MAMMY'S BLUEBERRY YUM YUM

KATIE, SARAI, and MARY JAXSON TRACY (Franklin, Tennessee) have a treasure trove of recipes from their great-grandmother, RUTHANNA MONGER (Sweetwater, Tennessee). Ruthanna was known to her eleven grandchildren as Mammy. Janet Tracy, her grand-daughter, was fortunate to inherit Mammy's well-worn, recipe book filled with close to one hundred of her time-tested favorites, many typed and others written by Mammy's hand. When the girls are old enough to be on their own, Janet looks forward to passing the recipes on to the next generation. The great-granddaughters especially love when their mom makes Mammy's Blueberry Yum Yum—mmm, mmm, delicious!

1/4 cup (1/2 stick) butter

1 1/2 cups graham cracker crumbs

1 (2.7 ounce) box whipped topping

mix, plus ingredients to make

1 small (3 ounce) package cream cheese, softened

1/2 cup powdered sugar

1 (30 ounce) can blueberry pie filling

---

1 In a small saucepan over low heat, melt the butter. Stir in the graham cracker crumbs.

2 In a medium bowl prepare the whipped topping mix according to the package directions. Add the cream cheese and powdered sugar and beat until creamy.

3 In an 8 x 8-inch square baking pan or a 9-inch pie plate, spread the buttered cracker crumbs on the bottom, saving 1/8 cup to sprinkle on top. Spread the blueberry pie filling on top of the crumb mixture. Then spread the topping mixture on top of the pie filling. Top with the remaining cracker crumbs. Chill approximately 4 hours until firm, or freeze. Serve cold.

MAKES 8 TO 10 SERVINGS.

CORNERSVILLE CRACKER TREATS ✕ ✕ ✕

JESSICA DILLARD (Lewisburg, Tennessee) says it's always a good time at her Granny LINDA ORR'S in Kingston Springs, Tennessee. She especially loves if they walk in and see Granny lying on the couch with her eyes closed. They'll ask her what she's doing, and her response is, "Oh, I'm just resting my back. I'm not sleeping or anything." Granny was born in Cornersville, Tennessee, and has been known to have a few memorable lines, including, "Right or wrong, good or bad, you're still mine," and "As long as I have a home, you'll have a home." Hosting an annual Mexican-themed Christmas party a week before the actual holiday is a tradition Granny started. Family and friends they wouldn't otherwise have the opportunity to see on the big day get together and dine on homemade Mexican food—chili with spaghetti and everything else imaginable—and to exchange gifts and celebrate Christmas with a twist! This generous Granny also makes sure anyone who is even considering coming has a gift under her tree.

---

1 (16 ounce) box club crackers	½ cup sugar (white or brown)	1 cup shredded coconut (optional)
½ cup (1 stick) butter	1 cup chopped pecans or walnuts (optional)	

---

1 Preheat the oven to 350 degrees. Line a large cookie sheet with the crackers.

2 In a saucepan over medium heat, melt the butter, add the sugar, and bring to a low boil. Sprinkle with the optional nuts or coconut. Remove from the heat and pour the butter and sugar mixture over the crackers.

3 Bake for 8 minutes. Separate immediately and serve.

MAKES APPROXIMATELY 16 SERVINGS.

MEMAW'S NO-BAKE CHEESECAKE

While brothers DREW, WILL, and SETH HELTSLEY currently live in California, they were born and raised in Tullahoma, Tennessee. They share that for every birthday growing up, their entire family would gather around Memaw JANICE COFFMAN EATON'S table in Tullahoma, for a group meal. Through the years, Memaw's cheesecake has been one of the requested birthday treats to end those family dinners with. This light, fluffy, lemony goodness is more like a pudding than a traditional dense New York cheesecake. The recipe Memaw uses is from the boys' great-grandmother (Grandma Eaton), Janice's mother-in-law.

CHEESECAKE:

1 (3 ounce) box lemon gelatin

1 cup hot water

1 (8 ounce) package cream cheese, softened

1 cup sugar

1 teaspoon vanilla extract

1 (12 ounce) can evaporated milk, chilled

TOPPING:

22 graham crackers, crushed

1/2 cup (1 stick) butter, softened

2 heaping tablespoons powdered sugar

1 TO MAKE THE CHEESECAKE, in a large bowl dissolve the gelatin in hot water and cool.

2 In a medium bowl use a hand mixer to beat together the cream cheese, sugar, and vanilla. Add to the gelatin mixture and mix together well.

3 In a separate medium bowl use a hand mixer to beat the evaporated milk until stiff. Add the whipped milk to the gelatin mixture. Spread into a 9 x 13-inch pan.

4 TO MAKE THE TOPPING, in a medium bowl mix together the graham crackers, butter, and powdered sugar. Spread over the cheesecake. Cover and chill in the refrigerator for 2 hours or until ready to serve.

MAKES 12 TO 14 SERVINGS.

CHATTANOOGA CHEW-CHEWS (A.K.A. TURTLES) ✕✕✕

ALICE TARUMIANZ was born, raised, and still lives in Lookout Mountain, Tennessee. She is known as Sissy to family and friends and as Sis-Sis to her six grandchildren. The youngest granddaughter, ALICE PERKINS (Nashville, Tennessee), was named in honor of her Sis-Sis. Chocolate chess pies, cookies, brownies, and these incredible turtle candies—Sis-Sis enjoys baking and candy making and can't wait to teach baby Alice when she's old enough to help stir; she's got licking the spoon down now, though. The older grandkids already love baking Christmas cookies with Sis-Sis and, of course, decorating them with lots of icing and sprinkles.

CRUST:

2 cups all-purpose flour

1 cup firmly packed brown sugar

1/2 cup (1 stick) butter (no substitute), melted

1 cup chopped pecans

CARAMEL TOPPING:

1 cup (2 sticks) butter (no substitute)

3/4 cup brown sugar

1 (12 ounce) package semisweet chocolate chips

1 Preheat the oven to 350 degrees.

2 TO MAKE THE CRUST, in a medium bowl mix together the flour, brown sugar, and butter. Press into an ungreased 9 x 13-inch pan. Sprinkle the pecans evenly over the unbaked crust.

3 TO MAKE THE TOPPING, melt the butter and brown sugar in a saucepan over medium heat. Bring to a low boil. Boil for 1 minute, stirring constantly. Pour the caramel mixture over the crust and pecans. Bake for 20 to 25 minutes or until the entire surface is bubbly.

4 Remove from the oven and sprinkle the chocolate chips over the bubbly top. Gently swirl the melted chocolate chips with a spatula to give a marbled effect. Cool at least 5 hours. Cut into squares. Out of this world!

MAKES 15 TO 18 SERVINGS.

SPECIAL SURPRISE "DIRT CAKE" ✕ ✕ ✕

CAROL ANN RUPP CRAWLEY (Alton, Virginia) raised four girls and one boy. Only son Scott is now a father to three boys and one girl. While Scott, wife Mary, and their children have recently relocated to Hawaii because of his career in the military, each of the four children is Southern born. In birth order, these Crawley grandchildren include ANDREW THOMAS (born in Knoxville, Tennessee), WADE ROBERT (born in Newport News, Virginia), and LAUREN ELIZABETH and GRAHAM DAVID (both born in Fairfax, Virginia). These four and Carol's other five grandchildren refer to her as Old Mommie. At Old Mommie's house they like to "pack" grandma's suitcase, blow bubbles outside, ride bikes in the country, catch frogs and insects, and build things out of boxes and paper. The grandkids love this dessert and always ask for more. They especially like the gummy worms hidden inside, so they advise when you make it you'd best put in plenty!

- 1/4 cup (1/2 stick) margarine, softened
- 1 (8 ounce) package cream cheese, softened
- 1 cup powdered sugar
- 2 (3 ounce) boxes instant vanilla pudding
- 3 1/2 cups whole milk
- 1 (12 ounce) container whipped topping
- 1 (1 1/4 pound size) package chocolate sandwich cookies, crushed
- 1 small (3.5 ounce) package gummy worms (optional)

---

1 In a large bowl cream together the margarine, cream cheese, and powdered sugar.
2 In another large bowl blend together the pudding, milk, and whipped topping. When well blended, pour into the cream cheese mixture and mix well.
3 Starting with the cookie crumbs, layer the cookie crumbs and pudding mix alternately, ending with the cookie crumbs on top.
4 For a fun surprise, stick several gummy worms in the mixture as you layer it and delight the grandchildren as they find the special critters hidden in their dessert. Chill in the refrigerator for 3 to 4 hours before serving. Serve cold.

MAKES 8 TO 10 SERVINGS.

GLENNA'S GRANDMA'S APPLE DUMPLINGS

GLENNA CHRISTY currently lives in Brookfield, Ohio, but she was born, raised, and lived in Pleasureville, Kentucky, the same town as her grandma, ELIZABETH BARTON. Glenna's dad was a farmer, and she and her parents lived with Grandma, who in her later years was cared for by Glenna's mother. Glenna shares that this dumpling recipe was made frequently when the green apples were available in the spring. It has been handed down in Glenna's family, becoming a favorite of her children and now her four grandchildren.

DOUGH:

2 cups sifted all-purpose flour, plus extra for rolling out the dough

2 teaspoons baking powder

I teaspoon salt

3/4 cup vegetable shortening

1/2 cup whole milk

6 small apples,* peeled and cored

Sugar, cinnamon, and nutmeg to sprinkle

Butter to dot each dumpling

SAUCE:

2 cups water

I 1/2 cups sugar

1/4 teaspoon ground cinnamon

1/4 cup (1/2 stick) butter, softened

1 Preheat the oven to 375 degrees.

2 TO MAKE THE DUMPLINGS, in a medium bowl combine the flour, baking powder, and salt. Cut in the shortening until the mixture resembles coarse crumbs. Add the milk and stir until the flour is moistened.

3 Roll into an 18 x 12-inch rectangle on a lightly floured surface. Cut into 6-inch squares.

4 Place an apple on each square. Sprinkle with sugar, cinnamon, and nutmeg. Dot with a small amount of butter. Moisten the edges of the dough, bring the corners to the center, and pinch the edges together. Place in a 13 x 9 x 2-inch deep baking pan.

5 TO MAKE THE SAUCE, in a medium saucepan over medium heat, combine the water, sugar, and cinnamon. Cook for 5 minutes, stirring constantly.

6 Remove from the heat and stir in the butter. Pour the syrup over the dumplings. Bake for 40 minutes until golden brown. Serve warm plain or with vanilla ice cream.

MAKES 6 SERVINGS.

* Good baking apples include Granny Smith, Cortland, Rome, Northern Spy, Pink Lady, or a mix of any of them.

CHOCOLATE COCONUT BALLS À LA NINI ✕ ✕ ✕

Grandson **PRESTON STROM** (Bellevue, Tennessee) shares that his Nini, **SANDRA MEADOWS**, and Papa come to almost all of the school activities and sporting events to cheer for him or his older brother and sister. Nini has four grandchildren total, and they all love birthdays and holidays, especially Christmas at Nini's house in Nashville, Tennessee. One of their favorite things to do is to make gingerbread houses that Nini then proudly displays as holiday decorations. This candy is one of Preston's mom's favorites, and she enjoys making it with Nini at Christmastime.

COCONUT BALLS:

2 (16 ounce) boxes powdered sugar

1 (14 ounce) can sweetened condensed milk

1/2 cup (1 stick) butter, softened

1 (3.5 ounce) can sweetened flaked coconut

2 cups pecans, chopped

2 teaspoons vanilla extract

GLAZE:

2 (6 ounce) package semisweet chocolate chips

1 (.25 pound) bar food-grade paraffin wax, chopped

1 TO MAKE THE BALLS, in a large bowl combine the powdered sugar, milk, butter, coconut, pecans, and vanilla. Mix well and chill 6 to 8 hours or overnight before rolling into balls.

2 When ready to prepare, remove the mixture from the refrigerator and roll into approximately 1-inch balls and place on a cookie sheet lined with wax paper.

3 TO MAKE THE GLAZE, fill a saucepan with approximately 3 inches of water and place a double boiler or large glass bowl over the pan. Add the chocolate chips and wax to the double boiler or glass bowl and melt. Keep the melted mixture over the hot water and with a toothpick dip each ball into the mixture. Let the excess drip off, and place the balls on wax paper to harden, approximately 10 minutes. Once hard, transfer the balls to the refrigerator and chill for at least 2 hours before serving.

MAKES APPROXIMATELY 3 1/2 DOZEN BALLS.

✕✕✕ CAROLINA PEANUT BUTTER CANDY

DESTINY "DESSY" CARPENTER (Waxahachie, Texas) shares that her Nana, LINDA LEDFORD PORTER, is proud to hail from the great state of North Carolina and a long line of precious, Christian ladies from Spruce Pine. And it's those ladies from whom Linda's learned so much. Linda recalls, "My granny (FLORENCE DELLINGER McKINNEY) and Momma (FRANCES McKINNEY LEDFORD) always made sure us kids were fed and made fresh cornbread and biscuits for every meal. They always had gardens and canned everything. I don't think they even owned a cookbook, making everything from scratch." Linda is a mother of four and a grandmother to six.

2 (16 ounce) boxes powdered sugar, plus extra for rolling dough

I tablespoon vanilla extract

1/4 cup whole milk, more if needed

I cup peanut butter

1 In a large bowl mix together the powered sugar, vanilla, and milk. Pour out onto a powdered sugar–covered countertop and knead until nice and smooth, approximately 5 minutes.

2 Using a rolling pin covered in powdered sugar, roll the dough to a 1/4-inch thickness. Spread with peanut butter; then roll up like a jelly roll. Cover with plastic wrap and refrigerate until firm, approximately 90 minutes.

3 When ready to serve, cut with a sharp knife into 1/4 to 1/2-inch slices and enjoy! Store uneaten pieces in the refrigerator.

MAKES 2 POUNDS.

SWEET POTATO DESSERT PUDDING X X

MARY BETH HEINE (Apex, North Carolina) shares that her grandmother, ELIZABETH WILLIS STANTON (Richmond, Virginia), was born and raised in Petersburg, Virginia, and was known to her grandchildren as Grandmommy. Mary Beth shares, "Grandmommy not only kept house, cooked, and took care of her aging relatives, but she was a partner in our granddaddy's furniture store for many of the years of their marriage. She showed her daughters and granddaughters very early on that you can be a wife and a mother and also work hard at another job. Additionally, she was an incredible artist who painted in oils for most of her life until she moved to a retirement home and used watercolors to keep the odors to a minimum. While I didn't inherit her painting ability, I admired that she used art as a creative outlet. Today, I sew and knit as a way of expressing my creative side while also working full-time in another field." Grandmommy passed away in 2003.

Butter to prepare dish	I tablespoon cornstarch	2 tablespoons butter, melted
2 large sweet potatoes	I whole medium orange	3/4 cup milk (whole or 2 percent)
2 large eggs	I teaspoon ground cinnamon	3/4 cup walnuts or pecans, chopped
1/2 cup brown sugar	1/2 teaspoon nutmeg	
1/4 cup sugar		

1 Preheat the oven to 350 degrees. Lightly grease a I 1/2-quart casserole dish.
2 Peel, then grate the sweet potatoes into a small bowl.
3 In a separate bowl combine the eggs, brown sugar, sugar, and cornstarch. Cut the orange in half and squeeze the juice from both halves into the large bowl. Add the sweet potatoes to this mixture and stir well. Add the cinnamon, nutmeg, butter, milk, and nuts and mix well.
4 Pour into the casserole dish. Bake for 50 to 60 minutes until the top is golden brown and the pudding is set. Serve warm, plain or with whipped cream.

MAKES 4 SERVINGS.

NOTE: *For variation, try adding 1/2 cup raisins and/or 1/2 cup shredded coconut before baking.*

Maw Maw **CLARIS BOND** was born, raised, and lived her life in Caddo, Alabama. Grandson **CHRISTOPHER PERRY HAMPTON** (Mount Juliet, Tennessee) remembers her as never having a harsh word for anyone and always being so patient, especially with them as children. He shares, "Maw Maw used to send us birthday cards with ten dollars in them. She was always smiling and seemed so proud of us. When I think of her, I see her smiling. Maw Maw always worked hard with all of the stuff that had to be done with my Paw Paw to keep the farm going; she strained the milk and churned butter. And I remember my brother and me tagging along behind her down to the barn to milk the cows or to gather eggs."

Vegetable shortening for preparing pan

I (14.4 ounce) box graham crackers, crushed

6 tablespoons margarine, melted

I (II ounce) package butterscotch chips

I (II ounce) package semisweet chocolate chips

I cup shredded or flaked coconut

I cup pecans, chopped

I (14 ounce) can sweetened condensed milk

1 Preheat the oven to 325 degrees. Lightly grease a 9 x 9-inch baking pan.

2 Press the crushed graham crackers into the baking pan. Pour the melted butter over the crackers.

3 Layer the butterscotch chips, chocolate chips, coconut, and pecans on top of the buttered crumbs in order.

4 Pour the milk evenly over all the layered ingredients and do not stir. Bake 25 to 30 minutes. Cool completely before cutting into bars.

MAKES 9 TO 12 SERVINGS.

✕✕✕ PINEAPPLE CASSEROLE

"Our daddy called her Mammy and we called her Grandma Smith," shares granddaughter **SARAH SMITH** (Tupelo, Mississippi) about **MARGARET SMITH** (Selmer, Tennessee), her paternal grandmother. Around the time of the Depression, Grandma Smith moved from Tennessee to Verona, Mississippi, after her husband passed away. They had twelve children, and when her husband passed, she was left to raise the three smaller children, the youngest of whom was just six months old. Times were hard for her, but she's remembered as a fine woman who took good care of her children all on her own. Money was scarce, so they appreciated everything they had and everything she cooked. Sarah loves this family recipe and adds that her cousin Estelle Goff (also of Tupelo) enjoyed making it as well before she passed away. It can be used as a dessert or tastes great as a side dish with ham or pork roast.

½ cup (1 stick) butter, divided

1 (20 ounce) can crushed pineapple

3/4 cup sugar

2 teaspoons all-purpose flour

1 cup shredded Cheddar cheese

1 sleeve round butter crackers, crushed

---

1 Preheat the oven to 300 degrees. Grease a 9 x 11-inch baking pan with 2 tablespoons of the butter.

2 Drain the pineapple, reserving 2 tablespoons of the juice, and spoon the pineapple into the baking pan.

3 In a medium bowl combine the sugar, flour, and cheese. Pour over the pineapple in the baking pan. Melt the remaining butter and combine it with the crushed crackers and reserved pineapple juice. Spread over the top of the casserole. Bake for 40 minutes, until heated well through.

MAKES 8 TO 10 SERVINGS.

GRANNY'S BEAR WIGGLE DELIGHT

AUSTYN CARPENTER (Waxahachie, Texas) shares that his Nana, **LINDA LEDFORD PORTER**, now lives in Swartz Creek, Michigan, but she was born and raised in Spruce Pine, North Carolina. Linda is a mother of four and a grandmother of six. Austyn's great-grandmother, **FRANCES MCKINNEY LEDFORD** (also of Spruce Pine), used to make this chocolate delight in the 1950s for her then "seemingly always hungry" six children. Linda says, "Momma would never believe that her 'Bear Wiggle' recipe is appearing in a twenty-first-century cookbook!"

---

3 tablespoons cocoa

I cup sugar

2 cups whole milk

I teaspoon vanilla
extract

4 ½ cups crumbled
leftover biscuits

---

1 In a medium saucepan combine the cocoa, sugar, milk, and vanilla. Cook over medium heat, stirring constantly until it thickens.

2 Place the crumbled biscuits evenly into 6 dessert cups. Pour the chocolate over the biscuits and lightly stir. Add your favorite ice cream or whipped topping and enjoy!

MAKES 6 SERVINGS.

HONEY'S PEANUT BRITTLE ✕ ✕ ✕

As a twentysomething young woman, KENNAH MASON (Franklin, Tennessee) considers herself very fortunate to still have a grandmother, let alone a great-grandmother! Her great-grandmother, BILLIE BUSHONG (Lewisville, Texas), is known to her grandchildren and great-grandchildren as Honey. Honey was born and raised in Mertvon, Texas. Kennah laughs as she shares one of Honey's memorable one-liners: "You can get happy in the same panties you got mad in." Kennah says the four generations of women in her family enjoy being in the kitchen together. Honey has made this candy every Christmas since she was about sixteen years old.

Cooking spray	1/2 cup water	1 heaping teaspoon baking soda
2 cups sugar	2 cups shelled raw peanuts	
1 cup light corn syrup		

---

1 Spray a cookie sheet.
2 In a medium saucepan over medium-high heat, cook the sugar, corn syrup, and water to the soft ball stage—238 degrees. Add the peanuts, stirring constantly. Continue cooking to the hard crack stage—300 degrees (when candy syrup dropped into cold water separates into hard, brittle threads).
3 Remove from the heat and add the baking soda. Stir until it turns golden brown. Pour onto the cookie sheet and allow the candy to expand itself; do not mix around with a spoon after poured.
4 Cool for approximately 15 minutes, then break into pieces. Store in an airtight container or plastic bag.

MAKES APPROXIMATELY 1 1/2 POUNDS.

Acknowledgments

Special thanks to my precious family—Chip, Chloe, Mia, Magnus,
and Kendal—for the countless hours you afforded me over
many long months to complete this labor of love.

Thanks also to:

Bryan, Joe, Margaret, Grandma Porter, and Grandma Ferkan

My mum, Charlotte, and mother-in-law, Nancy

My Nashville-based, monthly GDC (Gourmet Dinner Club)
cohorts: Violet, Mandy, Susan, Terri, Laura, Anne, Amy, and
the occasional guest (established in 2005 and counting!)

Relations old and new, and all the others in my life and in this book
who have shared with me their joy of cooking, baking, and entertaining

My nieces—Sophia, Olivia, Ava, and Lillian—may you
always know the love of family and good friends

About the Author

Prior to 1997, Faye had visited certain Southern cities either for vacation or en route to another destination for work or fun. However, in May 1997, two of her three brothers relocated to Nashville, and her love affair with this part of the South began. After missing her brothers and visiting them often, Faye decided it was time for her to relocate as well. While it took a while for a Chicago-based girl to find a Tennessee job, by January of the new millennium, she had made a fresh start in Nashville. And the rest, as they say, is history. Faye says she has never looked back and has never, even for a minute, second-guessed her decision to move south.

The warmth and welcome of the people, the hills, and the lush green surroundings remind her of Pennsylvania, where she was born. And the food? In the South, comfort food abounds. Faye shares that what tickled her most was her first trip to a meat 'n' three. "A what?" she remembers asking when a Southern coworker (now a great friend) invited her to lunch. She was amazed by the food. It was just like a childhood Sunday dinner at Grandma's—real down-home cooking at its best—but it was offered seven days a week. And the best part was that in the South, macaroni and cheese is a vegetable! (Many restaurants of the meat 'n' three persuasion list it under the vegetable selections.) Faye knew that her food life couldn't get much better than that.

Faye's background includes more than twenty years of experience in communications, marketing, and education-related capacities in corporate and nonprofit settings. She is the author of *At My Grandmother's Knee*, published in 2011 by Thomas Nelson. Her publishing background also includes managing editor roles for *MyBusiness* magazine (published by the National Federation of Independent Business) and *Real Estate Issues* (a commercial real estate journal published by the Counselors of Real Estate). Faye is currently the executive editor of *The Source* magazine and the director of education and communications for Middle Tennessee–based HealthTrust. She's married to none other than a Southern gentleman (of course), and together, with three dogs, they make their home in Nashville.

Index

·Contributor Index·